HORSES

Their Life in Pictures

Beatrice Michel
Photography by Lida Jahn-Micek

PAGE 1
The stallion is the
main contributor in
the establishment
and preservation of
social groups.
Through his
behaviour he also
influences the social
relationships within
a group.
(Andalusian
stallion in Spain.)

PAGE 2
Horses are not
loners. When they
are independent of
humans, they form
small groups.
(Andalusian stallion
in Spain.)

PREVIOUS PAGE
Horses are animals
of flight. With a fast
gallop they try to
leave any source of
danger behind
them as quickly as
possible. (Haflinger
in the Tyrol.)

This edition produced exclusively for
Smithbooks in Canada,
by the Promotional
Reprint Company Limited,
Deacon House, 65 Old Church
Street, London SW3 5BS.

Edited by Linda Doeser Publishing Services
Translated by Dominik Kreuzer

ISBN 1 85778 012 4

Printed and bound in Hong Kong.

Horses are nosy. Sudden noise, unknown objects or strange smells attract their attention. (Andalusian stallion in Spain.)

OVERLEAF
Early summer not only means warmer days and more succulent grass, it is also the season of births, rivalry and mating. (Andalusian stallion in Spain.)

Two four-year-old
stallions from the
Camargue greet
each other.
Emulating adult
stallions, they have
already adopted an
imposing posture.

CONTENTS

THE
FAMILY

ost people think of horses as solitary animals that graze alone in small meadows. In places where horses roam free, however, they live quite differently. Whether in North America, Australia, Japan or Europe, horses left to their own devices form groups, rarely choosing to live independently of others. A group of horses is not, as may appear at first sight, just a random collection of animals. Horses live in small families, called 'harems', which are always led by a stallion. Each of these stallions has one or two, sometimes even three, mares. The mares' foals and their one- and two-year-old offspring are also part of the harem. The adult members were born to another group and joined the harem later in life

The social behaviour of the individuals within the group is determined by a set of rules. The adult animals form relationships with each other, each knowing the others, and being aware of their strengths and weaknesses. Disputes between members of a group are controlled by a social hierarchy, headed by the leading stallion. The mares recognize his leadership and obey him when he adopts his characteristic driving posture to keep them together and lead them in a particular direction. The special position of the stallion is not only

reflected in his role as leader, but also as father of the foals that are born to his harem. However, the terms 'leading stallion', 'father' and 'social structure' are not completely adequate for describing the relationship between the adult members of the harem. Animals belonging to the group do much more than simply share living space; they are friends and partners. Their affection for each other is expressed through their closeness to each other, their greetings, physical contact and grooming. Once fully established, the relationships between the various adults within a harem last throughout their lifetimes.

In natural conditions, the birth ratio of female to male animals is about 1:1; in other words, an equal number of male and female animals are born. As each adult stallion has more than one mare, this leads to an excessive number of stallions, who then organize their own, secondary groups. Groups of 'superfluous' stallions constitute this second characteristic grouping of horses. Two- to four-year-old stallions usually spend their youth in such groups, joined by the occasional young 'guest' mare. These groups could be thought of as 'waiting rooms' for future leading stallions.

There are few species in which adult animals form lifelong relationships. These include some predatory animals, such as wolves and hyenas, and apes, such as macaques and gorillas. Among hoofed animals – a group that includes horses – it is rare. In most hoofed species, such as bison, buffalo and reindeer, only the mother and her young stay together and then only as long as the young animal is dependent on her care. Once it has become self-sufficient, they go their separate ways. The males of these species seek contact with the females only during the mating season. Some establish a claim to a territory during this time – an area of their choice, defended from other males. They

A small family of horses in the Camargue, consisting of the leading stallion (right), a mare and her foal.

wait there for rutting females. In some species, such as deer or zebus, mothers and daughters stay together, forming matriarchal families. This affords the daughter a number of advantages: in her mother's presence she is less likely to be driven away by other adults and is, therefore, able to feed for longer periods of time without interruption. She also occupies a more central position in the herd and so attracts less attention from predators.

It is surprising that among the six closely related equines still alive today, only the real horses – the Mongolian wild horse and the domestic horse – as well as the prairie zebra and the mountain zebra live in harems. The Asian and African wild donkeys, the mule, the domestic donkey and the Grevy's zebras live only in mother/offspring pairs, occasionally with an older offspring also remaining with the mother. Animals of all ages and both sexes come together in larger groups for hours or even days. They also form herds which, in the case of the Grevy's zebra, can comprise several hundred animals. In temporary groups, such as herds, animals come and go as they please; they are not bound together in any long-lasting way either by rule or relationship.

Unlike these other animals, which form only occasional and temporary groups, horses have a highly-developed social structure and so must meet different demands. A stallion has to defend himself against rivals, even when he is not defending his territory. Mares, on the other hand, must learn to live together harmoniously and respect each other. Foals learn how to establish their place within a group from their experience with other members of the harem. Finally, before young animals can themselves become adult members of a harem, they must cut the ties with their immediate families, form relationships with their peers and gain the experience they will one day need to be a leading stallion or a mothering mare.

This is how horses live...

OVERLEAF
What appears at first sight to be a mere collection of Camargue horses is, in fact, several families which have all chosen the same place to sleep. At longer rests, during which the horses also lie down, the members of a family stay close together.

In breeding establishments, such as the Szilvasvarad stud farm in Hungary, mares and stallions are kept apart. A group consisting of only mares, such as the one in this picture, never occurs in natural conditions.

OVERLEAF
Unlike their relatives
the donkey, horses
like to enter the
water, whether to
avoid the muddy
water at the edge of
a drinking place or,
like these
Andalusian mares,
to get at the
nutritious reed.

EVERYDAY
LIFE

FEEDING

The history of the horse began about 60 million years ago, with its ancestor eohippus. This literally means 'dawn horse'. *Eos* is the Greek word for dawn and also the term used to describe the eocene, the era during which it lived, and *hippos* is the Greek word for horse. Eohippus had four toes on each forefoot, and three on each hind foot, with a small, nail-like hoof on the tip of each toe. In those days, this small striped animal, which was no larger than 30-40 cm (12-16 inches), lived in the huge tropical rainforests of the old and the new world, feeding on leaves, fruit and seeds. When, with the changing climate, steppes and grassland gradually replaced the rainforests, the early horses adapted to this new environment. The change from being leaf-eaters to feeding on grass, together with the development of single hooves, was probably the most important step in the evolution of the horse. Because of its high content of coarse fibre, grass is a less easily digested source of nutrition. The teeth of a leaf-eater would not have been able to cope with it; only the evolution of the animal's molars, making them larger and coated with dental cement in the hollow areas of the enamel, enabled the consumption of harder, fibrous food without excessive wear. The large intestine increased in volume to become the dominant part of the digestive tract. There, with the help of microbes, fibrous vegetation is broken down. Because the structure of the digestive tract has adapted in this way the horse is able to live on a large variety of different foods available through the year. These include grass, foliage, fruit, which has a high sugar content, and seeds, which are rich in oil.

A Württenberg stallion from the Marbach stud farm in Germany supplements his daily fare with leaves and small twigs. Only eventually, in the course of evolution, did the adaptation of teeth and digestive system allow the switch from eating leaves to eating grass.

Ruminants, or animals that chew the cud, such as cows and oxen, can digest plants with a high fibre content, less nutritious protein and smaller amounts of sugar more efficiently than equines. A horse makes up for this drawback through selective grazing and with a higher daily intake of fodder – food passes through its digestive tract twice as fast as that of a ruminant. Looking at the wide range of ruminant species still in existence today and their large numbers compared to horses, one has to assume that, thanks to their superior utilization of food, they have spread at the horse's expense.

The food requirements of the horse have changed little since its domestication around 4000-3000 B.C. The first domestic horses still had to make do with grass which varied in quality according to the season. Later, when horses were not just ridden, but required to carry heavy loads and pull carts, fodder became a more important issue. The higher performance expected of them increased their energy requirements; their limited digestive capacity meant that grass and foliage alone were no longer sufficient. Furthermore, the time available for feeding was reduced. With the advent of crop cultivation the versatile digestive system of the horse was put to good use. The addition of barley, oats and rye to the horse's staple diet of grass, hay, straw and foliage increased its performance and, at the same time, reduced feeding times. Neither the structure and function of the digestive tract nor the feeding pattern have changed since domestication; small feeds between periods of rest correspond to the natural feeding rhythm of the horse, which has to find its own food in the wild. It feeds for periods of two to four hours and rests for an hour before feeding again. Depending on the quality of food, feeding takes up 12-16 hours of the day and is spread out evenly over day and night. On average, horses spend 60 per cent of their time feeding, 25 per cent resting and the remaining 15 per cent on other activities, such as dustbathing, walking, drinking and upkeep of social relationships. Depending on the season and the individual animal's gender and age, these percentages can deviate considerably from the norm. In winter, horses spend less time grazing and are generally less active. Yearlings, who are growing very rapidly and so require plenty of nourishment, and pregnant mares, who have to provide nourishment also for their developing foetuses, are particularly dependent on the availability of food in sufficient quantity and of quality. Despite prolonged feeding periods, lactating mares will usually lose up to 15 per cent of their normal bodyweight by the end of winter because of the poor quality of available food. Stallions can afford to be more active than mares, especially in spring. They rest just as much, but spend less time grazing. In general, young animals rest more than older ones, the very youngest spending the most time at rest. The foals are also the most active of animals and spend much of their time at play and exploring their surroundings.

During the day, horses are usually seen grazing in the morning or late in the afternoon. However, in the heat of summer, when they are plagued by insects, they often prefer to graze at night. Then, the cooling air and humidity keep

Horses in the wild spend between 12 and 16 hours a day grazing. In spring, stallions, like this Andalusian, have less time for grazing than the other members of their families because of the exhausting mating season.

OVERLEAF
Young Haflinger stallions enjoy a summer's day on an alpine pasture in the Tyrol. While grazing, they face in the same direction so as not to lose sight of anything.

Compared to bovines, horses are ten per cent more selective in their grazing. Leaves, fruit, herbs and bark from trees and shrubs enrich their daily diet. (A Lippizaner stallion from Hungary.)

the insects at bay, leaving the horses hours of uninterrupted grazing. In bad weather they face away from wind or rain. They seek refuge in preference to feeding only when weather conditions become extreme. While grazing, they walk slowly forward, making sure that they never stray too far from the group. They bite off blades of grass with their front teeth, usually just above ground level, lift their heads after several bites, chew and swallow while observing their surroundings, then lower their heads again. If grass is in short supply or covered by a thick layer of snow, they can rely on foliage, fruit and the bark of trees or shrubs, but only to a limited extent. In addition to the leaves of willow, aspen, beech and bramble, they will also eat gorse, holly, chestnuts and acorns, and sometimes they will dig for edible roots with their front hooves. They will also dig through snow to get to the vegetation underneath, choosing an area that is exposed to the wind because its covering of snow is shallower.

Camargue horses are exceptional in that a large part of their diet consists of the reed that grows in the widespread marshes of their habitat. They eat it as long as it remains green, but show a special preference for the young shoots that appear in early spring and have barely reached above the water's surface. They stand in the water for hours, nostrils partly submerged, to feed on their annual treat. Intensive grazing of the marshland results in a massive reduction of reed growth and a consequent enlargement of the free water surface. This benefits some other animals and provides an ideal resting place for migrating birds; some birds even spend the winter there. The cleared area also enables other plants, which the horses do not eat, to grow. These provide food for resting or overwintering ducks. Marshlands on which horses are kept tend to see an increased population of egrets, mallards, teals and coots. In this way, horses contribute to the enrichment and maintenance of the fauna and flora of this unique ecosystem.

Lactating mares have a particularly high nutritional requirement, as they also have to provide sustenance for their foals. (Asil Arab from the Olms-Hamasa stud farm.)

DRINKING

Horses need to consume a large amount of water. This is necessary for two reasons. First, it aids proper functioning of the bowels and of the animals' metabolism; after feeding, water containing certain secretions flows into the digestive tract. The less digestible the food, the more water is required. Second, water is essential for the control of the horse's body temperature. The amount required varies depending on how much is lost through sweating, given off via the lungs and kidneys or used to produce milk. To make up for dissipation of fluid during hot days or physical exertion, horses need to increase their intake of water. Although they prefer fresh, clear water, they often have to make do with brackish, polluted or slightly salty water. To avoid the dirt stirred up by hooves at the edge of a watering hole, they will wade towards the middle of the pond, submerging themselves as far as their bellies. Looking up regularly while they drink, they are always ready to flee from danger. Mares are more cautious than stallions. The ones that look up most often when drinking are also the ones that interrupt their grazing most readily to take flight at the slightest sign of danger. No particular animal seems to take on the role of leader on the way to or from a watering hole, although an older horse – either the leading stallion or one of the mares – usually heads the group. On arrival, it is usually the leading stallion who signals that it is safe to stay. He is also the first animal to drink.

Mothers of young foals, who require an increased intake of liquid for the production of milk, rarely stray far from a source of water. Grevy zebra stallions take advantage of this fact by establishing their territory around a watering hole. Mares, who become receptive again shortly after giving birth, will already be close by, ready to be courted and covered. Other stallions are permitted to drink, provided they are submissive to the owner of the territory. Mares are always given free access to it and young receptive females may attract the attention of the territory owner. Zebras drink at least once, often twice a day, usually in the morning and afternoon. In areas where they are hunted, they only drink at night. During the wet season they are less reliant on water, and may not seek a watering hole for two to three days in a row.

LEFT
Perhaps this English thoroughbred mare is testing the depth and temperature of this puddle with a view to rolling in it when the other mares have finished drinking.

On hot days horses not only drink more than usual, but also try to cool off by spraying themselves with water. (Hungarian half-breed mares.)

OVERLEAF
In cold weather horses move close together when resting. On such days they also avoid lying down. (Tyrolean Haflinger.)

SLEEP & REST

Adult horses usually sleep standing up and rarely lie down to rest. This probably reduces the danger of being surprised by predators. One animal of the group is always awake keeping guard. Furthermore, lying down and getting up again seems to require a great deal of effort for older animals. When an old animal has laid itself down and does not stand up, it is close to death. In one case, a very old Camargue mare who was unable to get up had to be put down. Sometimes an animal gets stuck when it does not have the strength to pull its legs out from underneath its body, for example in a small ditch. A foal, on the other hand, being much lighter and more agile than an adult horse, will usually sleep on its belly or flat on its side with its legs outstretched.

Horses avoid lying down on cold or wet ground. They fall into deep sleep only when they are lying down and wake up from such a sleep in gradual stages. During deep sleep, their sensory perception is dormant. They also appear to have some kind of dreams; they make noises – occasionally even 'snoring' – and their limbs twitch.

The members of a group are well co-ordinated in their activities. If one animal lies down or rests after grazing, it is quickly joined by other members of the family. Foals lie down beside their mothers and their older siblings take their place on her other side. Leading stallions prefer to doze next to their

This Haflinger foal from Vorarlberg in Austria rests its chin on the grass while he sleeps. Foals lie down more often than adults.

favourite mares. On cold nights, the animals move close together and at sunrise all activities are interrupted when the horses present their sides to the first rays of sunshine to warm their stiff limbs. On hot summer days, they seek refuge either in the shade or in areas that are exposed to the wind and free of vegetation. They spend most of the day there to avoid being attacked by insects, not so much resting as lying down repeatedly, rolling in the dust, swishing their tails and rubbing themselves against each other. Standing next to each other, facing front-to-back, they brush each other's heads with their tails to fend off the horseflies. Foals, in their desperation to escape these irritating pests, even put their heads between the rear legs of their mothers.

In the Camargue, a haven for insects, all the harems spend the hot midsummer days together. Leading stallions even tolerate the close proximity of rivals during this time. This closeness is to everyone's advantage, as the insect stings are spread out over a larger number of animals. As well as sucking a surprising amount of blood, the horseflies, which are about 2 cm (³/₄ inch) in length, are transmitters of numerous diseases. Solitary animals are stung more often than animals in a group and darker animals also attract more insects.

RIGHT
Although this thoroughbred Arab mare of the Beeghum stud farm in Austria is lying down to rest, her cocked ears show that she would jump up at the smallest disturbance.

OVERLEAF
Lying flat on the ground, legs outstretched – this is how foals prefer to sleep. Perhaps this little Lippizaner from Hungary is dreaming of playing with his chums.

GROOMING

Physical comfort is an important part of a horse's daily life. The mouth, teeth and front edges of the hind hooves are all used for cleaning and grooming the horse's coat.

Despite their relatively rigid backs and limited ability to stretch their legs sideways, horses are surprisingly agile when they need to scratch their heads or behind their ears. Balancing on three legs, their heads lowered to the ground, they are able to reach these areas with ease. All horses like to roll in sand, on dry, vegetation-free patches of ground or in snow. Before rolling, the animal walks around the patch several times, head lowered to smell the ground and scratching it to test its suitability. Then it lies down to rub one side of its body, swings out with head and neck and, with jerky, bending and stretching movements, rolls on to its other side. This activity invariably has a 'contagious' effect on other horses, which will soon join in. Mares in the later months of their pregnancy and old animals find it difficult to roll over and usually get up after rubbing one side to lie down again on the other. Some animals love to roll in mud, which may sometimes lead to comical situations. A Camargue stallion, whose coat was caked with a dark layer of dirt after a mudbath, ran towards his mares. On seeing him, they panicked and took flight. Puzzled, the stallion looked at his mares, who, with quickened breathing and cocked ears, were cautiously observing him from a distance. Only when he whinnied did his mares realize who they were actually looking at. Very young foals, who have never witnessed a dustbath, sometimes run away from their mothers when they see them rolling in dust. When they have rolled or are thoroughly soaked,

This Lippizaner foal is already struggling more than his contemporaries to scratch his back. Such places are best reached in pairs during mutual grooming.

LEFT
A Lippizaner stallion from the famous Austrian Piber stud farm tries to scratch his chest using his incisors.

OVERLEAF
Rolling on the ground helps to get rid of the thick winter coat in spring and enables this Shagya-Arab mare to defend herself against insects in summer. The foal has to evade the kicking legs of its mother.

horses shake regularly. This shaking movement begins at the head and then continues along the length of the whole body to the dock or fleshy part of the tail – a strange experience for a rider!

Most horses like to wade in water. They hit the water with their front legs, spraying themselves all over, but roll only in shallow puddles, if at all. Horses are good, powerful swimmers with a lot of stamina. Their relatives, the donkeys, on the other hand, exhibit a severe dislike of water. Even the smallest water-filled ditch presents them with a serious hurdle, which they will far sooner walk around than paddle through.

Horses nibble themselves with their incisors wherever they can reach – chest, fore and hind legs, belly and dock. They require the assistance of a friend,

The horse uses its head and neck to roll over on to its other side. (Top to bottom – a Haflinger mare, her foal and a Frisian stallion from the Krefeld stud farm in Germany.)

however, for the areas that they cannot reach. Using a distinctive facial expression, a horse will invite a friend to a social grooming session. If the other horse accepts the invitation, they scratch the tops of each other's heads and their withers, before working their way across the whole back and rump to the dock. This form of grooming is particularly common in spring, when horses need to rid themselves of the loose, itching hair of their winter coats. They often nibble each other for up to ten minutes without interruption. This behaviour also serves to strengthen their bonds of friendship. Mares and their foals usually groom each other. So, too, do brothers and sisters, young animals of the same age and leading stallions and their favourite mares. It appears that grooming also has a soothing effect on young animals.

During the moulting season and when plagued by insects, such as flies and ticks, a horse will rub itself against any firm surface it can find, including another horse. Insects that settle on a horse's ears, eyes and chin are removed by the horse rubbing its head against its own extremities. Using the dock frequently for this purpose usually results in worms. Standing next to each other, horses rub their foreheads against each other's shoulders and chests, and their lower jaws and throats against each other's backs. Often a passing animal will push itself under the neck of a bystander to brush insects from its neck and back – a method which is very popular with donkeys. It is also used by donkey stallions to block the path of a subservient male and prevent his approaching a rutting female. To fend off insects from back or belly, they throw back their heads, mouths closed, or quickly pull one rear leg up against the belly. Actively twitching individual muscles in the skin, swishing the tail and heavy stamping are also used to fend off pestering insects. Other horses, any inanimate object and the wind are the only defences a horse has against insects. Even insectiverous

A Camargue stallion enjoys a sandbath. These areas in the meadow gradually increase in size with daily use.

birds merely use the back of a horse as a convenient resting place, perhaps warming their feet on it in winter. The birds search for their food – insects that have been disturbed by the horses – on the ground and will even walk between the legs of the grazing animals. These sorts of birds have become a regular sight in the Camargue only over the past 30 years. More recently, other birds that are not insectiverous, have been observed imitating their behaviour. They also perch on the backs of the horses, but unlike their role models, they actually pluck loose hairs from the horses, which they then use to line their nests. The horses endure this plucking with stoicism and they may even welcome it. Only young foals dislike it and try to rid themselves of their passengers.

OVERLEAF
Demonstrations of rank between stallions always begin with postures to impress, which show the strength and elegance of this Asil-Arab from the Olms-Hamasa stud farm. A similar posture, albeit less distinctive, is used when courting a mare.

RIVALS
AND HIERARCHY

Andalusian stallions demonstrate their strength to each other on a Spanish beach.

The stallion of a harem and his mares are grazing peacefully in a valley. Suddenly, another stallion appears on the horizon. The first stallion looks up and observes the intruder. They walk slowly towards each other, stop at a respectful distance and stare at each other again. One of the two paws at the ground, smells an old dung heap, excretes over it and then watches the other copy this behaviour. Both return to their mares, who have, in the meantime, peacefully continued grazing – end of confrontation.

If one of the two is not deterred by the imposing posture of the other, he challenges him. With the powerful thrust of his hind legs, the reaching out of his foreleg and the slightly bent neck, chin proudly held against his chest, this stallion is reminiscent of a dressage horse in extended trot. How many riders know that this elegant movement is derived from the intimidation tactics of a free stallion who has seen a rival and is heading towards him in this posture? The ensuing confrontation is no less impressive than the imposing trot, but not as dangerous as may be thought. As if in slow-motion, their necks bent, the two stallions face each other, approaching until their nostrils meet. Moving slowly forward, they touch and smell each other's flanks and dock area. Now and again, with a kind of squeak, they jerk up their heads and stamp the ground with a foreleg. A ritualized show of strength, a demonstration of rank is in full swing. The confrontation usually ends rather less impressively than the way in which it started. One of the horses smells and paws at a dung heap, makes a few steps forward and excretes over it. Depending on the reaction of the other horse, it now becomes apparent which of the two is the higher ranking. If, after both horses have smelled the heap, one of them excretes over it again, he is the dominant animal and the subservient stallion trots off. The important symbolic nature of this action manifests itself in the fact that, when there is no dung in sight, the horses excrete on a heap of soil or rabbit droppings. Sometimes, presumably because their bowels are empty, they do not excrete at all and simply mime the action of doing so.

When a stallion has proved his status in combat and has conquered mares, he then has to be able to keep them. Frequently herding the mares helps to keep them together. Through his exclusive claim to the mares, however, every other stallion becomes his rival and he has to prove himself against them. If food, water and mares are abundant, stallions and their harems share their living space. Since they are liable to meet frequently, they have to find a way of living together despite their rivalry. To fight at every encounter would be too dangerous and the risk of injury far too great. By developing a means of demonstrating their rank, they appear to have found a way of defusing their encounters and controlling their co-existence. This enables stallions that know each other well to forego the customary greeting

TOP
Before determining their relative ranks, these horses try to intimidate each other with a 'canter of pride'.

BOTTOM
Their excitement rises as these horses sniff each other's flanks. They squeal and each lifts up a front leg and scratches the ground.

Rearing, pushing, tossing their heads and chasing – the game has started. Playing at fighting – horse-play – is the most popular pastime among young stallions and serves as a practice for the real situation. It also helps to determine the strengths and weaknesses of contemporaries.

ceremony; excreting or not excreting, is sufficient to indicate their relative ranks. It is no longer necessary to determine which is the stronger of the two. The stallion which is higher in the social hierarchy merely adopts an imposing posture and excretes occasionally to confirm his position as head of the family. Ownership of mares is the true status symbol of a stallion.

Sometimes, however, two stallions share a harem. Their relationship with each other is also subject to a hierarchy, which determines which one of the two may copulate with the mares. Thus, the hierarchy among stallions not only controls the co-existence of different groups, but also operates within a group.

Biting during a 'playfight' looks more dangerous than it actually is.

The purpose of these rules also becomes apparent in connection with other matters. For example, when water is in short supply and a number of harems have to share a watering hole, status within the hierarchy determines the order of access. Larger groups are dominant over smaller ones and can chase them from the watering hole or stream. As two stallions together jointly own more mares than a single stallion, these groups are at an advantage. If a large group approaches a watering hole, smaller groups often retreat voluntarily. If demand is great, smaller harems may have to

wait for a long time – often as much as five hours – before gaining access to the source of water. The distance of the harems from the watering hole, as well as the order of the harems while they are waiting, reflects their positions in the hierarchy. Single mares or stallions have to give way to all harems before being allowed to drink. Confrontations can occur when two closely ranked stallions want to drink at the same time. They threaten each other, rear and try to drive each other away. The mares actively support their stallions in such confrontations, biting and threatening to kick the mares of the other harem.

OVERLEAF
A Camargue stallion whose mating has been interrupted tries to gain some respect by stamping his front leg.

Not every encounter between stallions leads to a dung ritual. Sometimes an inferior animal avoids conflict through evasion. Even the rules of excreting are not always strictly adhered to. The leader of a harem sometimes forgoes excretion on meeting a young stallion and may even permit an inferior stallion to excrete over his dung. However, if a young stallion does not accept defeat when a leading stallion covers his heap, a fight ensues. This situation arises when a bachelor wants to take one of the stallion's mares. His success does not depend on size or strength alone; other skills, such as the speedy evasion of hoof-hits and the ability to reach his opponent's vulnerable head, throat and legs with his teeth or hooves, are just as important.

The tussles and playful fights between young stallions probably serve to practise these skills and may also establish a provisional ranking, which will partly determine their future social lives as leading stallions. Being at the top of the hierarchy is not only advantageous where access to water and feeding grounds and defence of sheltered locations are concerned. Leading stallions have at least two mares and are able to defend themselves against much younger rivals. In effect, this means that they are the most successful in terms of reproduction, fathering more foals than any other stallion. In general, the sons of higher-ranking mares seem to stand a better chance of attaining this status than those of lower-ranking mares.

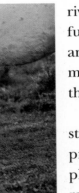

Two established leading stallions are sniffing a dung heap. It is not yet known whether the excrement of a horse carries its individual scent, like the urine of dogs.

Social hierarchy is not only important in the life of a stallion, but also plays a role among mares. Their position primarily decides priority at the drinking and feeding places. No complex rituals are required to assert their rank; laying back the ears is sufficient to put a subservient mare in her place. If she does not make way, she risks a painful bite or kick from the hind hooves of the challenging mare. Within a family of horses, the oldest mare is almost always the highest-ranking one, retaining this position for many years. Her offspring also benefit indirectly from her position. A mare with a suckling foal requires about twice as much protein as a mare without a suckling foal. When food or water are in short supply, the mare's rank can decide the survival or death of her foal. Only the mother's good physical health guarantees a supply of milk of sufficient quality and quantity. Furthermore, higher-ranking mares allow their foals to suckle longer than the usual seven to eight months before weaning. Sons of high-ranking females appear to gain the better prerequisites for a high position during their time in a bachelor group.

This inherited advantage does not apply to daughters, however. A young mare takes the lowest-ranking position at the start of her years of motherhood, regardless of her mother's rank. It also makes no difference to her position in the social hierarchy whether she chose to leave her family to join another group or was chosen by a stallion.

A playful fight between an older stallion and a younger one, whose coat is not yet completely white. By rearing, both try, in turn, to avoid the attempts of the other to bite their throats, while at the same time getting into a better position.

If two Camargue
stallions run into
each other without
warning, they do
not have time for a
careful approach in
a posture designed
to be imposing.
Rearing and
herding together
their respective
harems defuses the
situation.

ESTABLISHMENT
OF THE FAMILY

Because of his dominant position, the leading stallion decides which individuals are allowed to live in his harem. Besides the herding of his mares, his characteristic behaviour includes sexual activity, friendly contact and grooming. His attention in these activities is directed mainly towards the mares, which ensures the long-term survival of the harem. Lack of offspring does not change his devotion. For example, one particular Camargue stallion stayed with his mare for years, even though an abortion had rendered her sterile. When a stallion is not defending a territory, he just keeps rivals away from close proximity of his mares. A demonstration of his strength and his imposing behaviour show other stallions that the mares are his. However, the stallion is also the motivator in the foundation of a new group. Every adolescent stallion has the desire to become a leading stallion. At times a hefty battle of rivalry is fought for the possession of mares.

PREVIOUS PAGE
Having given birth, this Camargue mare is desirable to young stallions. Her leading stallion, who is greeting her with his imposing posture, will not move from her side during this time.

A Camargue stallion signals to his newly attained mare that she is no longer able to return to her old harem.

Established leading stallions do not take every available opportunity to acquire a new mare. If, for example, a lost mare stumbles upon a harem, the leading stallion of the group chases her away. For bachelors or former leading stallions, who are always on the look-out for mares, it is different. They have a number of ways of acquiring mares. Their success depends on the method they employ. Deposing a leading stallion, and hence taking over a complete group, is certainly the most dangerous. First of all, the leading stallion has to be very old and weak, injured or ill. To drive a leading stallion from his harem requires considerable courage, skill and strength, which bachelors have not yet acquired and former leading stallions no longer have. In addition, successfully deposing a leading stallion can cause other problems for the new owner of the group; the conquered mares join forces against him. Although, in normal circumstances, mares show aggression only towards other mares or young animals, they will reject this newcomer. They will kick him and refuse to accept him as their leading stallion. Only the lowest-ranking mares quickly adjust to the new situation. The stallion has no choice but to put up with the rebellious mares. To gain the upper hand, he herds them continually, biting them if necessary, in the hope that this will break their resistance. His future as leading stallion depends on his ability to establish himself as head of the whole group. The smaller the harem, the greater are his chances of success. If his new harem contains several mares, some of whom fail to accept him, he can usually keep just one or two, leaving the others to another stallion.

Another tactic involves 'creeping in'. A bachelor chooses a harem that is led by a weak or injured stallion and approaches the mares. When he is attacked by the leading stallion, instead of confronting him, he takes flight, only to return to the mares minutes later. This situation can last months, until the vigour with which the older animal defends his mares noticeably diminishes. As a result of his constant proximity, the mares gradually get used to the young stallion. Whether he chooses to chase the leading stallion away or just to take

Whether a stallion is able to keep a newly conquered mare and defend her against rivals depends on the level of his experience.

one or two of his mares, he stands a very good chance of becoming their new leader because of their gradual acceptance of him.

Females on heat present the most direct and promising opportunity for obtaining mares. The chosen mare must still be young, however. An older mare on heat, who, through year-long membership of a harem, has become an inseparable part of that group, will vehemently resist any young, inexperienced stallion's attempts to steal her away. On the other hand, young mares who leave their families during their oestrus are easy prey. The behaviour of young zebra mares on heat is said to be so distinctive that they are recognizable as being receptive from a long distance. They attract the attention of all bachelors in their vicinity. However, bachelors can also be very choosy.

Their attention is directed towards young mothers, who have just given birth for the first time. They seem to prefer mares which have already proved their reproductive ability. The risk of encountering a determined defensive stallion during an attempt to steal such a mare is greater than the risk he would take if he were to try for a 'teenager' on heat, but not as great as if he tried to steal an older, well-established mare. Younger mothers in a harem are not protected by the stallion to the same extent as the older mares and not at all if he is their father. A good opportunity for a bachelor is when a young mare, whose foal is still struggling to keep up, falls some distance behind the group. On discovering her, he rushes towards her and tries to drive her even further away from her group. This usually attracts other bachelors, who also approach. The young mother defends herself with teeth and hooves against these unknown animals who are trying to keep her away from her group. At the same time she has to protect her foal from being bitten or kicked in the fight which now breaks out among the stallions. If the mare escapes her ardent suitors, the young stallions usually have to give up. The mare and her foal flee back to her group. The young stallions, meanwhile, decide, on neutral ground, who is to

LEFT
A fight between
two Camargue
stallions, who
both lay claim to
the mare in the
foreground.

become her new owner. They engage in all available means of combat. Age, experience and also courage and determination decide the outcome of the fights. An older bachelor who plans to form his own family usually fights with more determination than an older stallion who merely wishes to add a mare to his harem. If a contestant succeeds in manoeuvering himself between his rival and the mare, he has a good chance of success. After a tiring combat, the defeated animal finally retreats. The victor has passed the first test on his way to becoming a leading stallion. Now he has time to deal with his new mare. If she attempts to return to her harem, he signals to her, with lowered head and laid back ears, that the way back is blocked. He does not move from her side and repeatedly tries to get close to her. The young mother, on the other hand, still tries to kick him. Patiently, he evades her attacks and increases his effort to make contact with her by means of friendly gestures. Her resistance fades very gradually and only after many days does it cease completely.

A pair of young stallions that have grown up in the same group of bachelors often form a close friendship. Such pairs also approach older mares that have just given birth. Two intruders are difficult opposition for a leading stallion; if he fights one, the other tries to separate his mare from the group. If he charges at that intruder, the other tries to steal the mare. Usually he has no choice but to give up the mare and round up his remaining mares to bring them into safety. From now on, this mare will have two leading stallions of which only one is actually in charge. Only the dominant of the two courts her when she is on heat, while the other attempts to keep other stallions away. It must be assumed that the subservient of the two stallions gains from this coalition by being able occasionally to copulate with the mare – an opportunity which would otherwise be denied this weaker and, therefore, presumably unsuccessful animal. This subservient position may also have long-term advantages; the lower-ranking stallion will later have the opportunity to leave with one of the mares or may take over the whole harem if his partner becomes ill or is injured. As the mares will already have accepted him, he will not have to assert himself against them in the way a newcomer would.

To a considerable extent, the balance of a newly-formed group depends on the experience of the new owner. Young stallions who have formed a family for the first time often lose their mares. If a young leading stallion loses in combat, he returns to live with his peer group of bachelors. Then, one day, strengthened and more experienced, he ventures out into the field again – this time, perhaps, with greater success.

OVERLEAF
When a mare and a
stallion have lived
together for a long
time, copulation
proceeds smoothly.
The foal, just a few
days old, is made to
feel uneasy by the
close proximity of its
father and makes its
submissive face.

SEXUAL
BEHAVIOUR

COURTSHIP & MATING

There are two phases in the oestrous cycle of a mare: the oestrus or heat and the dioestrus or the period between two cycles. Receptiveness lasts, on average, about five to eight days; from the end of a mare's heat to the next oestrus is 18 to 27 days. After giving birth mares quickly become receptive again – as a rule within seven to 11 days. Poor physical condition can delay the oestrus by up to 20 days. Mares are not receptive all year round, only at particular times. Their first cycle usually begins early in April when the days get longer. Among other things, the amount of light received by the eye triggers the start of the cycle. It affects the pituitary gland at the base of the brain, which regulates the release of sexual hormones. If, for some reason, the mare is not covered by the end of August, she does not become receptive again until the following spring. This limited period of receptiveness prevents pregnancy later in the year. A late birthday would reduce the foal's chances of survival; foals are born 11 months after conception.

After only a few weeks, colts begin to take interest in the excrement of their mothers. Having smelled it, they pass their own urine over it.

The first signs of heat shown by one of his mares attracts increased attention from the stallion. If the mare begins regularly to spread her hind legs and lift her tail, holding it to one side, she will soon be receptive. For the time being, the stallion restrains himself, only trying to approach the mare to sniff her rump, while nickering quietly. He is cautious because he might still be rebuffed by the mare. If he crowds her and tries, for example, to put his head on her croup, he risks being kicked. He is particularly interested in her urine, which she passes more frequently during this period. He tests each of her urinations, after which he fleers or makes a characteristic grimace. On the second or third day of her heat, the stallion becomes more active. He greets the mare more frequently with a posture designed to impress and with a typical noise which lies somewhere between nickering, squealing and puffing. Now, when he smells her genitals, she responds by lifting her tail and pushing her rump against his chest. He touches her flanks and neck with his nose and nibbles her legs and belly. This enables him to determine her readiness. If she is not ready, she will buck, squeal and run off. If, however, she turns her head towards him, touches his nose and allows his courting behaviour, he puts his head on her croup and mounts her. This courtship and the ensuing copulation occur several times a day when the mare is at her most receptive, usually after a prolonged period of rest. Young mares often appear to be somewhat coy and tend to make the stallion wait longer than older mares.

As the stallion is in the constant company of his mares, he is able to judge exactly when they are on heat. As ovulation takes place near the end of the oestrus and because the stallion's sperm is fertile for only two days, degenerating rapidly inside the mare's vagina, she needs to be mounted frequently to ensure conception. Thanks to the stallion's obliging nature, the mare is almost certain to be fertilized. Horses in the wild have a success rate of 95 to 98 per cent; in other words, only two to five mares out of 100 do not become pregnant. The rate of conception on a stud farm is much lower. For the English thoroughbred, for example, it is 40 to 70 per cent. One reasons for this lower rate is that, as mares and stallions are kept separately, the breeders have to observe and correctly interpret the mares' signs of heat. However, this does not necessarily correspond with the ideal time of reception. It is also possible that the forced and artificial nature of the situation has an effect on the chances of conception. Certainly the horses' sexual behaviour in this situation is severely limited. The two partners are led towards each other by hand and hardly have time to get to know each other. The time allowed for courting is reduced, being inhibited by manipulation – for example by putting a muzzle on the mare or tying her limbs. The rituals of courtship may even be completely done away with by the management of the stud farm.

In the wild, mares usually show no particular interest when their stallion copulates with another mare. However, jealousy between two mares has been observed. The mares were receptive at the same time, the higher-ranking one pushing and kicking the stallion when he was was mating with the other mare.

If the mare has a young foal, it stands beside her while she is being courted and mounted. The unaccustomed closeness of the stallion seems to unsettle him, however, and he frequently adopts a subservient expression. Yearlings, on the other hand, try to keep courting stallions from their mothers by repeatedly pushing themselves between the couple and bucking against the stallion. Particularly adamant youngsters have to be put in their place by a bite from the stallion. After all, their own mother is of no sexual interest to them.

Stallions take their time when they are courting a mare. By sniffing this Lippizaner mare from the Szilvasvarad stud farm, the stallion is able to ascertain whether she is ready for mating.

OVERLEAF
For the time being, this stallion keeps his distance from the mare. Her attentive face and forward-pointing ears declare her readiness for coupling.

Instead, they try their luck with others. Even if the stallion of the harem does not intervene, they are unsuccessful because the mares themselves will fend them off. Sometimes more mature youngsters, who have not yet joined a group of bachelors, still play at protecting an older mare on heat. If the leading stallion wants to copulate with her, he meets more resistance than he would with a yearling. The young animal lays back his ears and presents his hindquarters to the leading stallion, ready to kick, while simultaneously adopting his subservient expression – a sign that he still accepts the older and superior stallion as higher ranking. Sometimes, the leading stallion will allow the young animal to copulate with one of his mares, although the chances of conception are very small. The ability of stallions of this age successfully to cover a mare is highly questionable – at least in the case of wild Mustangs. Their sexual organs are not fully developed until they are three years old, by which time they will, of course, have left their families.

The stallion is able to test whether the mare is in oestrus by means of certain substances in her urine. It is no surprise, therefore, that the stallion shows an interest every time the mare urinates. The stallion also tests the urine of his mares outside the reproductive period. He smells both their urine and dung, frequently fleering afterwards, and passes water over them. This behaviour is seldom displayed by mares. It is interesting to note that the behaviour of a stallion towards urine and dung changes as he grows up. Adult stallions, for example, pass water more often than young ones, more frequently covering the waste of others. The ability to control the amount passed, and hence the ability to urinate more frequently, seems to be developed only in adult animals. Leading stallions do not cover just any waste with their urine, but almost exclusively that of their own mares, although they do test the excretions of

The lifted tail, held slightly to one side, indicates the readiness of this mare to mate.

other mares. This leads to the assumption that they can distinguish the waste of other mares from that of their own. How often and, more specifically, whose waste is covered depends not only on the age of the animals, but also on their social position. A young stallion, up to the age of two, who still lives with his family, covers both his mother's waste and that of the other mares of the harem. If he is taken into a new harem, he ceases to take an interest in the waste of the mares of his former harem, including that of his mother, concentrating, instead, on that of the new mares. This behaviour enables both old and, probably,

In his excitement, this Lippizaner stallion rears up, beside the mare, in an impressive posture with his neck bent and his chin held against his chest.

young stallions to express their relationship with certain mares. Young stallions do not appear to be scared off by the presence of another stallion's urine on the dung or urine of a mare, even though this suggests that the mare is already accompanied by a dominant stallion. The common interest of old and young stallions in the same waste often causes them immediately to approach the place at which a mare has passed her waste and urinate over it. Disputes about superiority and demonstrations of ownership are not at issue. A young stallion is not prevented from covering waste by either his father or another stallion of

In natural herds, the act of copulation is repeated many times in the three to five days during which the mare is in season.

the group. After both animals have sniffed the waste, the older horse not only permits the younger to urinate, but sometimes even gives him priority. Young stallions are equally tolerant of each other, queuing up to pass water over a dung heap. Young, 'homeless' stallions that have left their families in search of a new group show no interest at all in the waste of mares. Older bachelors, on the other hand, that live in groups of their own without mares, often search for mares' dung heaps or urine, sniffing the ground like dogs. They smell each area carefully and fleer – this tells them a great deal. As stallions are in the habit of depositing their waste over dung heaps near watering holes and alongside paths, choosing the same places each time, large and conspicuous dung heaps eventually accumulate in these places. When young or leading stallions encounter such places, they can determine whether other animals frequent the area and how long ago they passed by. Places at which a harem has rested are also revealing; as animals usually pass their waste after a prolonged rest, mares on heat may be discovered.

PREGNANCY

Towards the end of a mare's period of heat, ovulation takes place. Pregnancy begins with conception – the fertilization of the ovum by a sperm – and lasts for about 336 days, that is, 11 months to within a few days. The duration varies slightly, depending on the age and breed of the mare and the time of conception. Older mares do not carry so long as young ones, thoroughbreds somewhat longer than cross-bred animals, and colts are usually carried a few days longer than fillies. Mares covered early in the year often carry longer than ones that mated later. It seems likely that good nutrition during the middle months of pregnancy can reduce its duration. Whether pregnant mares go full term depends on a variety of factors. For one thing, the age of the mare is decisive. Up to the fifth year of their lives, mares give birth to fewer foals than in the following years. In a healthy environment, two-thirds of young mares give birth; in less than perfect conditions only about half do. This is probably related to nutrition. It is known that a lack of protein in the third to fifth week of pregnancy can lead to a miscarriage. It is also easier for a pregnant mare to complete her pregnancy within a stable family. A forced change resulting from theft by another stallion deprives a mare of much of her strength. In addition, integration into the new harem involves coping with the aggression from the other mares. Finally, as newcomers always take the lowest place in the hierarchy, they also have to make do with food of lower quality.

According to Arabic horse-breeders, the pregnant body of a mare is a treasure chest full of gold.

During the first six months, the foetus develops relatively slowly. After 150 days, for example, it measures a mere 20 cm (7¾ inches). At that stage, all the organs are present, albeit not fully developed, and the foetus weighs 3-6 kg (6½-13 lb). In the following months, it grows quickly, gains weight rapidly and its coat begins to develop. At birth, the foal will weigh 30-60 kg (66-132 lb) and measure 75-145 cm (30-57 inches) from head to dock.

The birth of twins is very rare among horses. There appears not to be enough room in a mare's uterus for the simultaneous development of two animals. At a certain stage of pregnancy, the competition between the two foetuses becomes so great that one of them dies, causing an abortion. If they are carried to birth, they are either stillborn or too weak to survive longer than the first hours of their lives.

At birth, a foal's living conditions change dramatically. For 11 months, he has been fed, cushioned and kept warm and safe. At birth, as at no other time in his life, is the demand to adapt to a new situation as great. He has to breathe, stand up while coping with gravity, maintain his body temperature within a certain range and excrete his waste products. Surprisingly quickly, he will master these skills without any problems and, with the help of his mother, eventually grow up to be a fully fledged member of his family.

OVERLEAF
A mare in the Camargue gives birth among the familiar members of her harem, who pay little attention to the event.

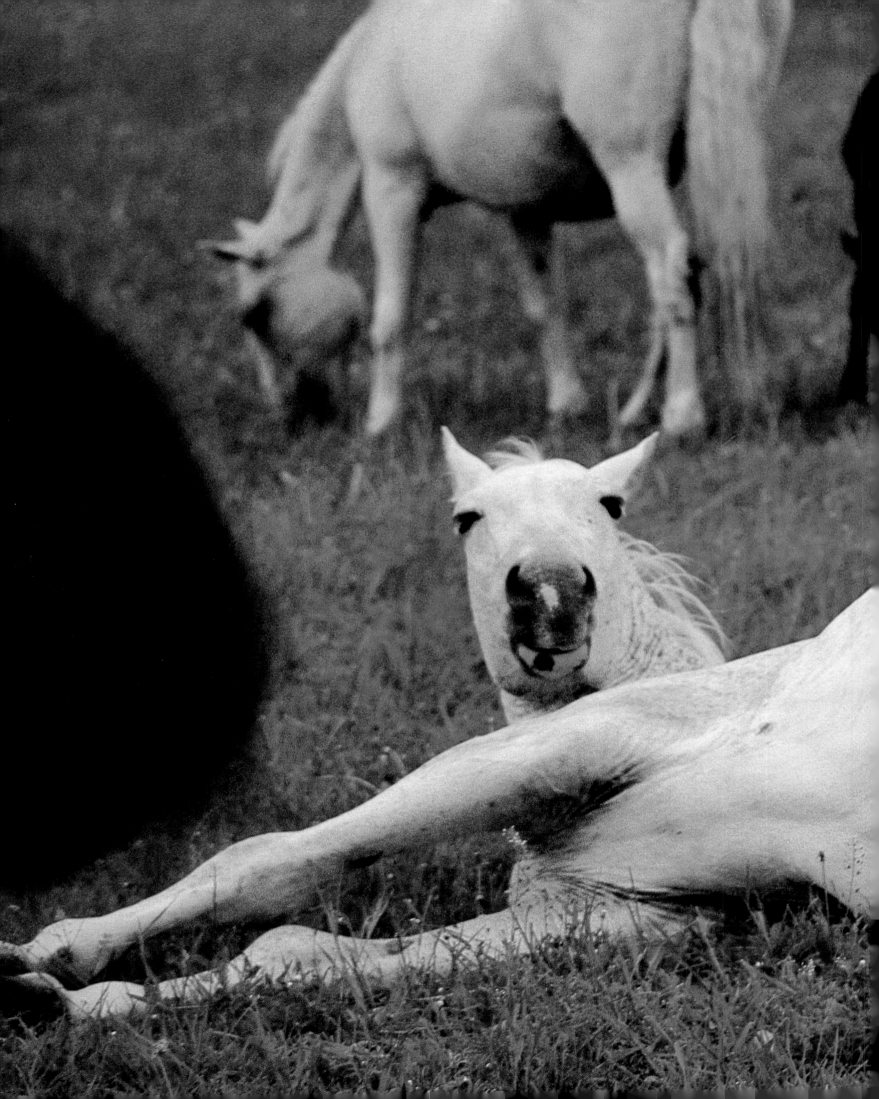

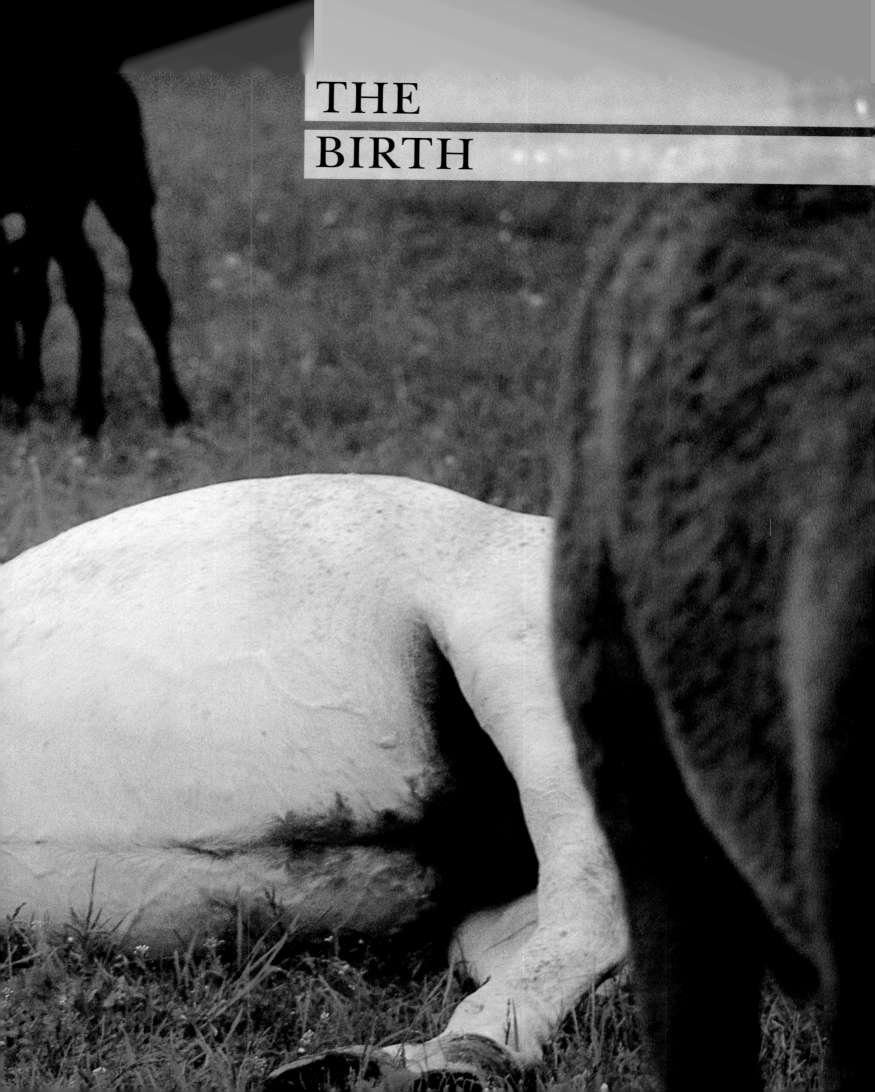

THE
BIRTH

In regions were there is extreme seasonal variation in weather conditions, the quality and quantity of food available varies considerably. It is, therefore, advantageous for a foal to be born at a time which offers the best chance of survival. In the northern hemisphere, most foals are born in spring, between April and June. The birth usually takes place at dawn, which is convenient in that it leaves the mother and her newborn all day to get to know each other and allows time for the foal to learn to stand up and follow its mother before the night sets in. To a limited extent, a mare can regulate the time of birth. Domestic horses tend to wait for darkness to give birth, when they will not be disturbed by stablehands and other people. In natural conditions, the mare remains with her family to give birth. She is surrounded by familiar animals, who pay hardly any attention to the process.

Various signs precede the birth. The udder swells in preparation for the production of milk. Sometimes small droplets of milk form on the teats. A swelling of the pudenda indicates multiple loosening of the pelvic tissue. The softening of the connective tissue, triggered by hormones, prepares the pelvic tissue, which will have to stretch during the birth. Immediately before the birth, the mare's flanks collapse slightly. This is caused by the foal's changing position in the uterus. Throughout the pregnancy the foal lies with its back downwards or to the side; when labour sets in, it turns on to its belly, its head lying on its legs and facing the cervix. Birth is imminent when the mare begins to become restless. At short intervals, she lies down, rolls, stands up again, paws the ground and carefully smells the place on which she was lying. She often looks back at her body and licks her belly. After the first contractions she lies down. The contractions push the limbs of the foal towards the cervix, thus widening it from the inside. The whitish-blue amniotic sac, which enclosed the foal in the uterus, breaks, allowing the amniotic fluid to escape. The pressure which the foal exerts on the walls of the birth canal increases the contractions which are supported by the contraction of the abdominal muscles. These muscular contractions are most effective when the mare is lying down. She lies flat on her side and stretches her uppermost rear leg so that it does not touch the ground. The foal's forelegs leave the uterus first, followed by the head, which acts as a wedge, allowing the shoulders to escape. The foal is still covered by the amniotic sac, which tears as a result of the pressure exerted on it or through nodding movements of the foal's head. The foal then takes its first breath. The birth takes an average of about 18 minutes. Mares giving birth for the first time usually take longer, even though their foals weigh less at birth than that of a mare who has given birth before. Exhausted, the mother lies on the ground. Her foal, wet and with drooping ears, is still lying in the amniotic sac. Its rear legs have not yet fully escaped. Its front hooves have soft, white pads on the undersides, which prevent damage to the mare's uterus and cervix during birth. This soft bone will soon fall off and the hooves will harden. The foal's

After a final contraction the whole body of the foal, apart from the hind legs, has been born.

The mother touches her newborn for the first time. It is wet, has drooping ears and is still lying in its amniotic sac. An older foal from the same group also greets the new arrival.

first breaths drastically increase the concentration of oxygen in its blood, giving the baby animal sufficient energy to move. When it has finally pulled itself free, it collects its legs under its belly and, with enormous effort, attempts to stand. To do so, it has to bend its hind legs and position them under its belly, while simultaneously stretching its front legs – a difficult task! As soon as the front end is up, the hind legs begin to wobble and collapse, and vice versa.

Meanwhile, the mare has stood up and, in the process, torn the umbilical cord at a place naturally designed for that purpose. She touches her newborn and carefully smells the amniotic sac and the ground. However, she neither eats the sac nor, later, the placenta. Nor does she help her foal to free itself from the amniotic sac; she merely touches and licks it, which encourages it to make further attempts at getting up. The intensive licking stimulates the foal's circulation and frees it of the amniotic fluid. It also helps the mare to familiarize herself with the smell of the foal. From now on, she alone will accept and mother only this foal. Adoption by another mare is unheard of in the wild.

The importance of smell in recognizing and accepting the newborn is illustrated by the example of two Camargue mares, whose behaviour stands in complete contrast with that of other mothering mares. Both mares gave birth

While the foal makes its first attempts to stand, its mother familiarizes herself with its scent.

to a foal in the same place within two hours of each other. Because each of them touched and licked the other mare's foal, both accepted both foals as their own. For three days after their birth, the foals were able to suckle both mares; however, after that, the mares appeared to be able to recognize the smell of their own foals and chased the other one away.

Through the foal's repeated attempts to get up, the amniotic sac slides off it. Eventually it manages to stand on all fours for a moment, before falling down again. It tries again – and finally stands, albeit very shakily and with its legs wide apart. Only 15 to 40 minutes have passed since its birth! Standing like this, it has more in common with a grasshopper than a horse. To keep its balance, it locks its front legs against the ground with the result that its first steps are likely to be taken backwards. Then it begins, slowly and shakily, to edge its way along the body of its mother, never breaking contact with her. Almost immediately, the foal is presented with the next problem – it has to find the udder. It looks in dark places that offer resistance to its mouth: between its mother's neck and chest or at the top of her legs. The mare stands still, occasionally touching the foal and perhaps nudging it towards her rear legs, where the udder is located. When it stands in the correct position for suckling – parallel to the mare – she nibbles and licks it more intensively. The foal stretches out its tongue and bends the edges upwards to form a channel. After many attempts, which take around 30 to 60 minutes, it finally finds the udder and suckles for the first time. This first nourishment, called colostrum, contains special proteins called antibodies, which protect the foal from certain infections. These are necessary as the newborn foal has no immune system of its own. As these antibodies can be absorbed through the walls of the stomach and intestines for only a short time after birth, it is of great importance that the foal suckles shortly after standing up. A delay of only a few hours can considerably reduce the level of immunization. After about two hours, the foal excretes the meconium, faeces that have collected in the bowels of the foetus.

With the first suckling, the mare not only ensures her foal's survival by securing its nourishment, but her behaviour guarantees its security and comfort.

OVERLEAF
Mothers do not let any other animal near the foal on its first day. This thoroughbred Arab from the Beeghum stud farm in Austria is fending off a young stallion who is a little bit too nosy.

On its first day, the foal suckles, cautiously tries to run, sleeps and explores its surroundings. Although it is now looking for milk in the right place, it does not always find it instantly. With every attempt, however, it becomes more adept, until it finally finds the teats at the first try. As soon as it has taken one of them into its mouth, it pushes the udder with its head to stimulate the flow of milk. A first-time mother may occasionally appear

surprised to find a little creature at her side. Sometimes, perhaps due to lack of experience or because her udder hurts when it is touched, she fends off her foal's first attempts to suckle. Generally speaking, a foal does not benefit from being the first-born. An inexperienced mother may not be able to protect it from injury when stallions are fighting over her. There is also the danger that she will not offer sufficient resistance a bachelor trying to take her and will go with him, deserting her newborn. On several occasions, a mare has travelled on with her harem, leaving her sleeping foal behind. These were always mares who had given birth for the first time and in their own families. As they spent their entire pregnancy with members of their families, perhaps their ties with their own mothers

ABOVE
Young foals are interested in everything that is around them. (Thoroughbred foal from the Beeghum stud farm.)

were still too great, or the ties with their foals had not yet developed sufficiently. A separation of only a few hours can lead to the mother's rejecting her foal. Lost or deserted foals have little chance of survival in the wild.

Not long after giving birth, the mother begins to graze again, frequently interrupting her feeding to touch her foal. While she eats, her baby explores its surroundings. It approaches strange objects, such as trees, shrubs and

Even on its first day the foal precariously gallops around its mother.

stones, and sniffs and nibbles them without fear. It takes leaves or small twigs into its mouth, shakes its head up and down and throws them up in the air. It already knows how to rub itself against a tree, the ground or its mother's body and how to scratch its own coat with its mouth. It can yawn and make its insecurity known with a distinctive facial expression. Shaking can still cause it to lose its balance and when its mother touches it, it sometimes falls over. If it tries to scratch itself with one of its hind hooves, it usually topples over. Even if it can manage to balance on three legs, the lack co-ordination between its leg and its head prevents it from scratching successfully. It merely waves its leg in the air to no avail.

This foal does not know the world yet, but its ears show that it wants to find out.

A foal often touches its mother and already plays with her on the first day of its life. It bucks and kicks, jumps up on her side or back when she is lying down, pinches her head or nibbles her mane. The mare patiently stays still or continues to graze. The first gallop takes place around the mother, no more than five metres (16 ft) from her. When she moves off, the foal runs beside her close to her head. If it cannot keep up, its mother waits or goes back to it. She walks around it and past it, encouraging it to follow her again. Confronted by obstacles, such as a ditch or a gap in the undergrowth, it often hesitates and stands still. If, despite encouragement from its mother, it does not dare to continue, the mother returns. If, after repeated attempts, it will still not follow her, she looks for a different route.

When the foal sleeps, the mare grazes close by. Any animal approaching her foal attracts her attention. Out of curiosity, it seems, the other members of the harem want to touch and smell the new baby. Yearlings are particularly interested, staring at the small animal again and again. The mare, however, thwarts any attempt by a stranger to make contact with her foal on the first day. She instantly intercepts and kicks any animal that tries to approach her young. This may be because it is vital that the foal familiarizes itself with its mother to prevent the possibility of its following another animal. A newborn foal would follow any large moving thing – another mare, a yearling, even a human being. Only on the second day is it able to recognize its mother, by smell and not yet by sight.

The foal could also be threatened by an animal which it approached. As it does not yet understand threatening gestures, it could receive a painful bite or kick. Young animals are more tolerant, showing a friendly curiosity towards it, but the mother has to keep higher-ranking mares at bay. Since these will, in general, reply with threatening behaviour and refuse to leave, the mother has no choice but to lead her foal away. She threatens and even bites animals with whom she normally has a friendly relationship, such as her yearling or her grooming partner. Even though she does not completely isolate herself, she avoids contact with all other animals on the first day of her offspring's life.

OVERLEAF
The smallest sign of danger causes this mare from the Beeghum stud farm to flee. Her foal, just a few hours old, stays close by her side.

LEFT
Shortly after
giving birth, the
mare begins to
graze again. After
all, she now has to
sustain her foal as
well as herself.

While the mother
affectionately
nibbles her foal, she
moves one hind leg
back slightly to make
her udder more
accessible.

On the first day the mother eats noticeably less than she does on the following days. She has to stand still for suckling, keep other horses away and follow her foal whenever it strays from her side. On the second day, she finds more time to feed. After all, she now has to provide for her offspring as well as herself. In the wild, mares with very young foals are nervous, fleeing at the slightest sign of danger, their foals following at their sides. However, they do not hesitate to attack predators. Zebra mares with foals have frequently been observed using their hooves and teeth to attack hyenas. Naturally, they were supported by the leading stallion, who never lost sight of his mare while she gave birth, and, indeed, had hardly moved from her side since.

OVERLEAF
Even though this
Lippizaner foal in
Hungary is older, it
never strays too far
from its mother,
who is the centre of
its life.

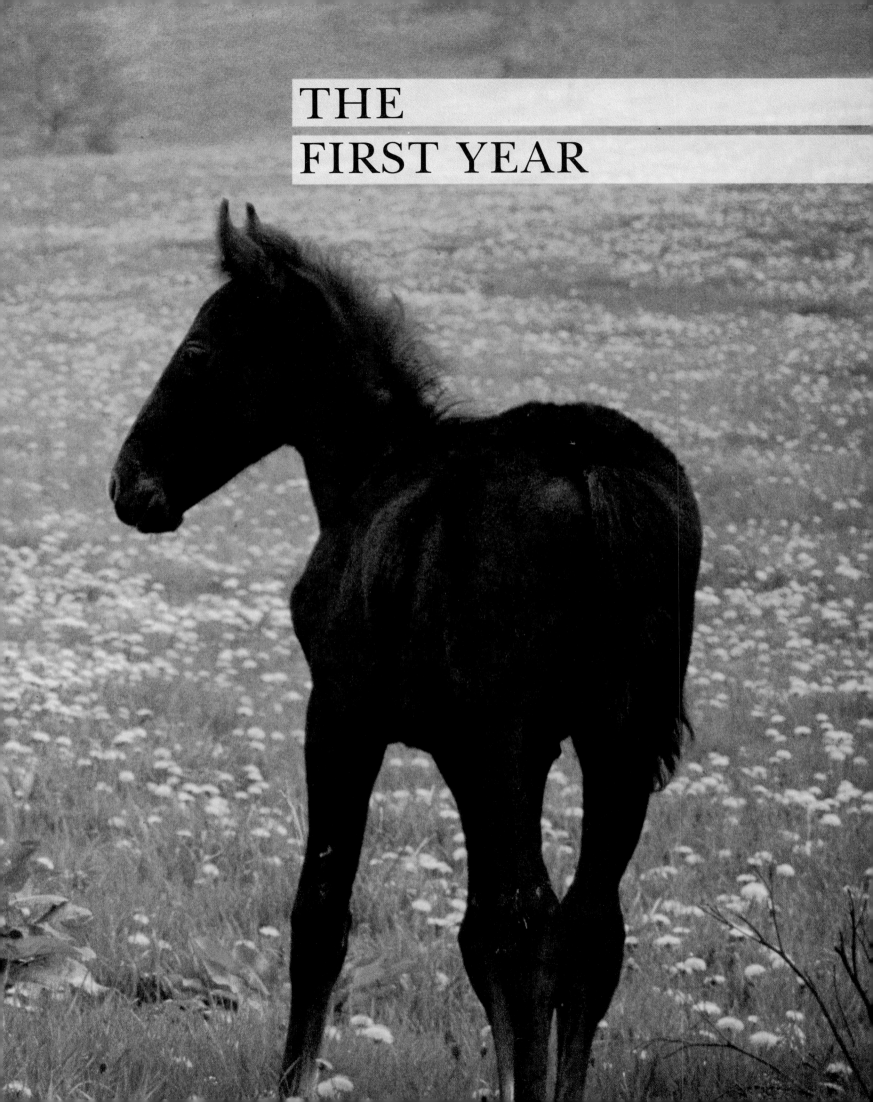

THE
FIRST YEAR

Horses are among those animals whose young follow their mother as soon as they are born and remain in close contact with her at all times. They are distinct from other hoofed animals who leave their young in well-hidden places, only occasionally returning to feed them. Animals that live in the steppe, such as wildebeest and zebra, have to be able to travel to other areas in search of food during the dry season. A young animal, therefore, has to be able to follow its mother and keep up with her so that the whole family can travel over the long distances necessary. In addition, the close proximity of the mother offers the foal protection from predators.

Spring in Spain – a beautiful day for this Hispano-Anglo-Arab foal to race about in this meadow.

A foal lies flat on the ground to sleep. Its mother stays close by, grazing in a circle around it, or stands beside it to rest. Her foal has to be at least eight weeks old before a mare will go farther off to graze with the other animals of her family in the usual way. In these circumstances, the foal wakes up to find itself alone or surrounded by strange horses. It raises its head and calls for its mother, who replies from the distance. It runs in the direction from which the call came and stops by the nearest mare. Hesitantly it approaches her, but her laid-back ears and swishing tail tell it that this is not one it is looking for. Another whinny from its mother indicates the right direction and it races towards her. By pushing itself under her neck, it forces her to stop; it rubs its head under her belly and, without hesitation, begins to suckle. The mother gives easier access to her udder by stepping back with her rear leg on the foal's side. She does not move away until the foal has finished. The mother is only this considerate of her foal's needs as long as it is

This Haflinger foal has jumped upon its mother, who is its first playmate.

fully dependent on her milk for its nutrition. To begin with, the milk is of exactly the right composition to provides the foal with sufficient nutrition. It drinks 150-250 ml (5-8 fl oz) about twice every hour. However, after a few weeks, the milk is no longer of sufficient quality or quantity and the foal learns to feed itself by copying the other animals. Although it already nibbles at herbs, grass and twigs on the first day of its life, it does not swallow vegetable food until the end of the first week, when its teeth have grown through the gums. To be able to reach the grass, it has to spread its legs apart, which, at the age of four months, is difficult – even for only 15 minutes a day. Older foals often still try to get to the udder. Sometimes both parties become downright insistent; if the foal pushes itself under its mother's neck, she pushes it aside and walks on. When it finally gets to the udder, the mother decides when it should stop suckling by raising her rear leg and running off. Foals become agitated by this premature termination of their feeding and react by laying back their ears and angrily bucking and kicking.

At mother's side the world can be explored in safety.

In its first month, a foal frequently eats its mother's fresh dung. This behaviour is by no means abnormal and has sound physiological reasons. The dung provides the foal with vitamins and single cell micro-organisms, which are vital for the normal functioning of its bowels. By the time it reaches three to four months, a foal will eat almost the same grasses and herbs as adult horses, although it spends nowhere near the same amount of time grazing. Milk still provides much of its nutritional requirements, although the quantity produced by the mare reduces after three or four months. This leaves the young animals more time for playing and sleeping.

As it becomes older, a foal sleeps on its side less often. Instead, it lies on its belly or dozes standing up. In order not to lose its mother, the foal now follows her with 'reeling' steps at short intervals. The responsibility for not getting lost is now the foal's. The mare will follow her young to lead it back to the family when necessary only for the first few days. After that, she tolerates separation over quite large distances, no longer showing concern every time the foal falls behind. Even though it sometimes mistakes a strange mare of similar size and colour for its mother, it is now capable of recognizing her on sight from some distance, and by her smell close by.

Apparently without any reason, a foal may suddenly start to run, stop abruptly and then gallop in a large circle around its mother. Experienced mothers continue to graze, merely following their offspring with their eyes. A young mother, on the other hand, is likely follow it and may intrude upon strange families, causing considerable excitement. Her stallion immediately tries to drive her back to his other mares, meets a neighbour who tries to herd his own agitated mares together, and finally the other foals catch on to the

OVERLEAF
The foal's mother offers not only milk, but also safety. (Arab in Andalusia.)

LEFT
Mother knows
where to rest on a
hot day – in the
shade. (Haflinger
foal in the Tyrol.)

excitement and start to run around excitedly. It takes a while and many calls from concerned mothers before each foal is back where it belongs.

Naturally, foals rank at the very bottom in the hierarchy. If they encounter adults, they are threatened or kicked, but it seems that older animals show consideration for the inexperience of the youngster. A kick from the hind legs is usually executed with little force – almost as gesture. The foals, on their part, enjoy a kind of fools' freedom. While adult animals respect their superiors and rarely dare to show aggression towards them, foals will direct their threatening gestures at older, more dominant horses. However, their threatening gestures, usually bucking and kicking, are mainly defensive and are not otherwise taken seriously; if they are, mother's social position provides due respect.

A foal observes with interest how its mother paws the sand, lies down and rolls. Even on its first attempt to copy her, it learns the benefits of a dustbath. Despite repeated attempts, however, it is unable, at first, to roll over on to its other side. It has to get up and lie down again to be able to rub both sides on the ground. Meanwhile, the others impatiently await their turn. If an animal pushes in, it is threatened or kicked by the foal. It feels triumphant about making the others wait, but this is really the work of its mother, who has signalled them to wait until her colt or filly has finished. It is, of course, advantageous to have a high-ranking mother; it enables her to offer it privileges such as this. Older foals can mingle with other members of the group without the direct protection of their mothers. On approaching another animal, a foal indicates its insecurity with a chewing gesture. If it is threatened, it reacts with the same expression. This, it seems, prevents stronger action if the foal does not immediately obey a higher ranking horse

Its mother is the centre of a foal's life. She offers protection and she provides food. From her side begin its little explorations, and at her side it learns to run. It is hardly surprising, therefore, that she is also its first playmate.

Foals have a lot of time to laze around, play and, above all, sleep. (Lippizaner foal in Hungary.)

OVERLEAF
As long as the foal is still small, its mother, a Camargue mare, always stays close by, even when it is asleep.

91

BROTHERS & SISTERS

One morning some time in spring, the young horse, by now a year old, suddenly finds a young creature at its mother's side. Surprised and curious, it approaches its new sibling to touch and smell it, but the mother blocks its path and chases it off with a painful bite. This happens every time it tries to make contact with the foal. She even shows aggression when it wants to approach or touch her. Luckily, this behaviour – inexplicable and frightening to the yearling but vital for the protection of the newborn – does not last too long. Under the careful supervision of its mother, it is allowed to touch the foal on the second day. As the days go by, the mare gradually lets the yearling approach her again and their relationship returns to its normal state. The yearling will still rest beside her, run to her when danger threatens and follow her when she walks off. However, the first place behind her is now occupied by the foal. The first meeting with the foal, too, holds a surprise for the yearling: the foal evades it and presses itself against its mother's belly and even kicks at it. If,

On excursions the foal is always the first in line behind its mother, followed by older brothers or sisters. (Family of Andalusians in Spain.)

94

however, the foal mistakes it for their mother and searches for the udder under its belly, it gets a friendly sniffing from the yearling.

Within a few days the foal grows used to the presence of its older brother or sister. Its curiosity often leads it to the yearling, whose friendly behaviour encourages increasing contact between the two. The little foal is particularly welcome when it shows a willingness to join in with social grooming activities.

After the first four weeks, the foal is at the side of its mother for only half the time, spending the rest of the day with its brothers or sisters, who are the first animals, apart from its mother, that it gets to know. Only then, does it make contact with its contemporaries. The more independence the foal gains from its mother, the closer its relationship with its siblings becomes. The yearling is now rarely chased off by its mother – usually only when the foal needs to suckle. She, presumably, does this to let her yearling know that the milk is exclusively for the foal. Nevertheless, it is said that exceptions prove the rule – some yearlings manage to trick their mothers and sometimes get to the udder by, for example reaching the teats through the mare's hind legs. In the case of a one-eyed Camargue mare, her yearling was able to suckle by approaching her on her blind side. These tactics are generally only successful when the foal suckles at the same time or when the mother is dozing or not paying attention. It is rare for the 'thief' to profit for long. Maybe its better developed teeth or the way in which it takes the teats into its mouth give the game away.

The bond between mother and offspring breaks only when the child leaves the family. (Thoroughbred Arab mare with foal and older daughter on the Beeghum stud farm, Austria.)

The company of its sibling furthers the foal's independence from its mother. It dares to leave her side at an earlier age than foals without siblings. By late autumn, the foal will spend as much time and have as much social contact with its brother or sister as it will with its mother. The arrival of yet another foal strengthens the bond between the two older ones even more. These friendships can become so close that, when the oldest offspring leaves the family, the next oldest follows it. Conversely, a yearling will not feel inclined to leave its mother if she does not give birth again or her new foal dies early in life.

PLAYMATES

At first the mare decides with whom her young is allowed to have contact. Initially, the foal itself runs from unknown animals and hides behind its mother. However, in order to fit successfully into the social structure of the family and the herd, it is essential that it gets to know the other members of the family. The preconditions for this are a lessening degree of maternal protection and an increase in the foal's confidence. Initially, it leaves its mother for only short intervals. Gradually it goes farther afield and leaves her for longer periods of time. Adult animals usually chase it away, but other foals welcome its presence. They form groups which graze, lie down and, most of all, play together. Differences between colts and fillies become apparent at an early age. While fillies take part in chases, they hardly ever fight with each other and only occasionally fight with colts. As fillies' involvement is somewhat passive, colts seek each others' company when they want to play. At only ten days old, they are already grabbing each other's necks with their teeth, playfully biting each other's legs, rearing and chasing each other to bite each other's croup. They strike out with fore and hind legs, suddenly fleeing only to return to confront their playmates again. The same behaviour – only rougher and resulting in a few scratches – can later be observed among young stallions. The early parts of the morning and evening are the usual times for play. A journey to the watering hole, another pasture or a resting place usually encourages play. After a prolonged period of playing, the foals usually return to their mothers, suckle and then, exhausted, fall to the ground and sleep. The older they get the more time they spend with their playmates, also grazing together. Nevertheless, when they want to rest, they still return to members of their families, preferring to sleep next to their mothers.

It is now autumn and the foal has grown. Its coat has lost its smooth appearance and is now thick and shaggy. It no longer has disproportionately long legs compared with the length of its body. Its muscles have developed through play and its rump has become wider. It can now confidently move about its herd and also knows other youngsters of the same age and older, as well as the members of its own family. The time has come to start out on the road to adulthood. The end of its childhood is signified by an event which is very unpleasant for the foal – being weaned off its mother's milk.

Only male foals play this energetically. (Haflinger foals in the Tyrol.)

LEFT
The older the foals become, the more important playmates are to them. (Young Dülmener in Germany.)

OVERLEAF
Biting the cheeks and legs is all part of the game between these Haflinger foals in Vorarlberg, Austria.

WEANING

As it gets older, the foal has an increasing number of unpleasant experiences; now, as soon as it approaches its mother's udder, it is threatened by her, even bitten. To rest or graze beside her is still permitted, but any attempt to touch her is rebuffed. Occasionally, it succeeds in procuring a small sip of milk from her udder, which, by now, is almost dry. The foal is about to experience its first conflict with its mother. All its attempts, even its bucking and kicking, are in vain – no more milk. The youngster now has to find its own nourishment. The highly nutritious protein it received in the milk is now missing from its diet and, at the age of eight months, it is in the middle of a period of rapid growth. To obtain the required nourishment and to reach half the bodyweight of an adult in the next four to six months, it has to find a lot of time for grazing – between 14 and 18 hours, depending on the quality of the food available. This is the same length of time as older, bigger horses. This means less time for sleeping, lazing around and playing with its companions. It gradually distances itself from its mother and spends much of its time grazing with other foals, who share the same fate. Its relationships with other animals, and especially the proximity of its mother, whose friendly contact is now increasing again, help him through this difficult time.

For orphaned foals life is harder. They may be seen standing at the edge, lonely and lost, leaning against a tree as if to draw comfort from it. Sometimes they even refuse to feed during the day. In natural herds homeless foals sometimes find 'foster mothers', usually relatives, such as an older sister or brother.

At the other extreme, there are comparatively fortunate foals, who are allowed to suckle for as long as eight months. This happens when the mare does not become pregnant the following spring and sometimes when the foal is the first born. In the former case, the foal may have the benefit of its mother's milk until it is 18 months old. Whether the mare is covered in the following year is of no significance – two years is the limit in any case. If the mare has given birth for the first time, the suckling period is extended for a further two months; a precious bonus for the foal, considering the lack of good quality fodder in the wild during the winter months. The grass not only lacks protein, but it is also dry. At least it fills the stomach; during that time, the foal's belly is often the only round part of its body. Cold nights, an early winter and a thick layer of snow stretch the foal's resources as much as poor quality food and the lack of vitamins, which restrict skeletal growth. Even the cuddly appearance of the foal, lent to it by its thick winter coat, cannot hide the fact that the first winter decides not just its physical development, but its very survival.

A hard time
begins for this
Dülmener now
that he has been
weaned.

After a hard winter, the arrival of spring is heralded by the lengthening days. At last there is sufficient grass again. To shed their winter coats, the animals rub themselves against trees and roll on the ground at every opportunity. Difficult-to-reach areas, such as the withers, the back and the croup, are freed of itching hair with the help of others. The young animals, by now a year old, generally choose grooming partners of their own age and take up their favourite pastime again – playing.

The difference between mares and stallions at play, already established at a younger age, becomes more apparent. Female yearlings may spend time with their younger siblings, but their activities can hardly be described as playing. They rub their heads on the foal's body, put it on their backs and with their chests push it along in front of them. The foals hardly respond to this 'game'. By contrast, the play of the stallions becomes even more energetic and intensive. Within their age group, grooming and playing are not the only activities, however; fights also break out. Instead of bucking and kicking – a mode of behaviour, incidentally, still shown towards older animals – they threaten and bite each other. A hierarchy of rank is in the process of being established, but, at this stage, it is by no means permanently fixed. Here, a difference between the sexes becomes apparent: young mares appear, at least at this age, to dominate their male contemporaries. The only animals certain to show submissive behaviour towards a yearling stallion are foals.

A male yearling still has close links with his mother, but shows increasing interest in his father. He often seek his father's company, showing his respect with a typical submissive expression. The stallion appears to have no interest in his son, although sometimes they groom each other or the yearling manages to encourage him to play a game. Yearling stallions show a greater interest in

In bachelor groups, fights to establish rank and hierarchy take place as well as 'playfights'. Threatening gestures, such as the one from this Arab stallion, are serious.

their fathers than young mares demonstrate. Mares and stallions play very different roles later in life. It makes sense, therefore, that their development in the second year of their lives follows different paths. They do have one thing in common, however: life becomes serious when they leave their families.

Most animals, besides young horses, leave their families, some of them long before their bodies are fully developed. These include prairie zebras, the young of the South American camel, guanacos and vicuñas. There are good reasons for this early departure from the familiar family. The adult males of all of these hoofed animals stay with their females all year round, defending them against other males. Their growing sons are, therefore, potential rivals although, as we will see later, they usually leave the arena of their own volition. In addition, remaining in the family can lead to inbreeding. Mating of close relatives – mother and son, for example – may result in weaker, less healthy offspring. This is equally true for daughter and father pairings, which could, genetically, have undesirable consequences.

Furthermore, if all daughters remained in the family, a shortage of food might result, which would, much to the detriment of the whole group, lead to increased rivalry among the mares. Not only the weakest would feel the pinch. The mares would frequently get in each other's way and would, consequently, not have much time to feed in peace. An increase in the size of his harem to this extent would make it much more difficult for the stallion to control and keep his group together. The risk of a mare falling behind and being taken by another stallion would also be greatly increased. All in all, enough reasons for animals to leave of their own accord – although young camels are not that considerate and have to be driven away by their fathers!

Until recently, little was known about young mares. Their development is more subtle than that of their male counterparts. Recent research, however, has shown that their lives are just as fascinating and that their path to adulthood may lead them in different directions.

THE YOUNG MARE

The physical development of the horse is by no means complete in two years. Although the rate of growth reduces in the second year, a horse is not fully grown until it is four or five. Ponies, primitive species and Camargue horses take as long as six or seven years to reach their final size. In terms of their social behaviour, however, mares are grown up long before they reach this age. Adulthood means motherhood and membership of a harem and mares are able to give birth at the age of two. As a rule, however, mares in natural herds do not begin to reproduce until the third year of their lives and wild horses, such as Mustangs, not until the age of four. Mares have their first fertile periods when they are 18 months old, although these are irregular and of short duration. Because they are not yet fully mature, the behaviour of the young mares in their first oestrus is not always recognizable as such and the period may pass almost unnoticed. They do not attract the same sort of attention that a fully grown mare receives from a stallion. If a mare mates during this time, it will be with a stallion of the same age, either from her own or from another group. Leading stallions from other groups also sometimes copulate with these mares, without taking them into their own groups afterwards. Her father pays little attention to the young mare. He makes no attempt to prevent other stallions from approaching her and does not take a stand against rivals, provided they maintain a respectful distance from his own mares. The young mare herself shows an unwillingness to pair with him, evading his attempts to approach her and showing her submissive expression.

Young mares often remain at the edge of the group. When they are on heat they go off to visit other harems. (Haflinger mares in the Tyrol.)

The first heat of a mare in her 'teenage years', therefore, rarely leads to pregnancy. The situation changes when the cycle commences the following spring. Whether it takes place at the first occurrence or after several cycles, the first time a young mare is covered is usually successful. In many cases, this event coincides with her departure from her family. The first signs of her impending departure become apparent some time before she finally leaves. She seeks less contact with her mother, who tolerates her presence without either paying much attention to her or chasing her away. A young mare often stays at the edge of her original harem, sometimes leaving her group for several hours, even days. She visits other harems, preferring those with other young animals. She keeps returning to her own family until, one day, she stays with the group of her choice. As the young mare is on heat at that time, she is covered by the

male members of their new group – the young stallions as well as the leading stallion. However, her integration takes time. The older mares are aggressive towards the newcomer, who is forced to take the lowest position in the hierarchy. The leading stallion does not pay much attention to her once she is no longer on heat; several weeks pass before he recognizes her as a member of his group and defends her from other stallions. Her choice of suitable partners is, therefore, limited to other young animals, in general mares, with whom she forms close links.

Some young mares take a different direction. They allow strange stallions to cover them – usually several different ones – without moving to another group. These mares spend a further 11 months with their families, by the side of their mothers and siblings. Their situation is finally changed irreversibly and dramatically with the birth of their first foal. Young bachelors, who have waited for an opportunity such as this, or older stallions intending to increase the size of their harems throw themselves at such a mare and try to take her with them. Whether her new owner will be a bachelor or a leading stallion is decided not by her, but by the outcome of a battle between the stallions.

Observing and understanding young mares takes patience, as their behaviour is inconspicuous. (Haflinger mare in the Tyrol.)

Whichever way a mare becomes a member of a new harem, she will be with that group for a long time, if not her entire life. If the stallion dies or is replaced by a younger stallion, the mares stay together and are taken over as a group by their new owner. Depending on conditions, she will give birth every year – and leave her growing daughters to go their own way.

THE YOUNG STALLION

Like mares, stallions grow slowly. Although they are physically capable of covering a mare at the age of two years, their career as successful parents begins later in life. Most stallions do not father a foal until they are five years old, by which time a mare of the same age will have given birth several times. In ideal conditions, mares can give birth every spring until they are 20 years old. The reproductive success of a stallion is not so predictable. Though they can cover several mares in any one year, the number of foals they father in a lifetime depends on factors such as the size and quality of their surroundings, the size of their harem, their ability to compete and the age at which they form their harem. A stallion will father most of his foals between the ages of nine and 11; after that the number reduces. However, as some stallions are very successful at that age, while others have a limited number of descendants and a few father no foals at all, this can be viewed only as a generalization.

Regardless of how old he is when he has the first mare of his own, how many he will have and how long he will be able to maintain his position as leading stallion, a bachelor's adulthood begins, as it does for a mare, when he leaves his family. The most likely reason for his leaving is prevention of incest. A direct reason for his departure is the change in relationship with his father. The fact that a young stallion will move on even if the leading stallion is not his genetic father supports the assumption that social mechanisms rather than genetic recognition of relatives are operating. The few cases of a brother copulating with his sister may be explained by the fact that the older brother had replaced the leading stallion of the harem of which his sister was a member; as he had left by the time she was born, he could not have known her. In the wild, such incidences are probably extremely rare because young stallions tend to travel a greater distance when they leave their families than young mares. A meeting with a relative is, therefore, a rare coincidence.

This group of bachelors would play just as vigorously in the wild. (Ponies in Germany.)

As the leading stallion becomes increasingly annoyed by the presence of his son, his threatening gestures increase. Sometimes he will attack the younger horse, despite its submissive expression. No young stallion can stand up to such an attack. He takes flight, closely pursued by the older animal, whose laid-back ears show that this is no game. In general, young stallions do not let it come to that, choosing, instead, to escape the growing tension in their family. The other reason for a young stallion to leave his family is almost certainly his desire to find contemporary companions. In the wild, young stallions some-times travel great distances in search of a new group. They are welcomed by other stallions who share the same fate – into so-called bachelor groups.

Bachelor groups comprise not only young stallions, but also former leading stallions who have been defeated and replaced or whose mares have died. A constant coming and going takes place in these groups; older animals leave the group to form a harem and are replaced by younger ones. Young stallions usually spend one or two years with a bachelor group; some stay longer. Close one-to-one friendships are sometimes formed, usually between animals who already knew each other perhaps having come from the same group. All mem-bers of a bachelor group have a friendly relationship with each other. They graze together peacefully, clean each other's coats and, above all, play a lot.

Another popular pastime among young stallions is demonstrating rank. Despite their friendship, there is a certain degree of rivalry, although fights will only break out once the stallions have started to look for mares.

Then, one day in spring, a mare gives birth – an opportunity for an older bachelor! Stallions who try to conquer a mare in pairs are no exception. If the attempt is successful, controlled conditions will exist in the new family. One of them is superior to the other and asserts himself by being the last one to deposit his dung on any heap. Apart from that, the role of each individual ani-mal is clearly defined; when a rival threatens, the subordinate stallion faces him, while the other brings the mare into safety. Only the dominant stallion has the right to copulate with her – or so one would assume – but it appears that the inferior stallion also fathers a foal with this mare from time to time.

This relationship does not always stand up to the constant pressures within it; demonstration of rank leads to fights and the weaker animal may eventually decide to leave. If the harem has, through successful co-operation, increased in size, the departing animal usually takes the lowest-ranking mare with him. So the stallion has reached his goal – to own one or two mares with whom he will be able to spend many peaceful years.

OVERLEAF
Young Lippizaner
stallions in a playful
chase.

HORSE-PLAY & COMBAT

In the course of playing at fighting, almost all of the techniques of serious combat are used – but with less vigour. Two stallions playfully begin to bite each other's cheeks, before aiming for the legs, neck and head. To avoid being bitten, they dodge their opponent and circle around him, or they simply place their rumps on the ground. To protect their forelegs they kneel. Now and again, to evade their opponent's attacks or to come down on top of him, they rear. This is followed by a chase, during which the animal being chased suddenly stops, wheels around and attacks and chases his pursuer. The intensity of play is indicated by the position of the ears and the facial expression: younger stallions play with their ears pointing forwards or sideways and their faces are relaxed, while older animals tend to lay their ears back and tense their facial muscles. 'Playfights' between older stallions can end up as serious conflict, particularly in spring. Numerous bruises are inflicted and, occasionally, one animal is lamed; this gives an indication of the intensity of these tussles. The stallions are, it seems, in a heightened state of excitement. It is now known that, in spring, a stallion's bloodstream contains a higher concentration of testosterone, a male sexual hormone, than it does in autumn or winter.

Playing at fighting is training for the real event. Bites to the opponent's head and neck and rapid turns followed by kicks can decide the outcome of a fight in seconds. (Young Lippizaner stallions.)

Like many other mammals, stallions play in order to practise their fighting tactics, getting to know their future rivals' strengths and weaknesses at the same time. This experience probably better enables them to determine the risk of losing a real battle and incurring injury. To distinguish between play and confrontation is not always easy for the casual observer and the transition from the one to the other can be seamless – a harmless scuffle can suddenly escalate into serious combat. Nevertheless, there are clear signs which distinguish play from fighting. A desire to play is indicated by a raised head and repeated nodding at the partner. The ears, although possibly pointing back slightly, are not pressed back against the head. Serious biting is replaced by gentle nipping and rank is of no importance – both animals play the role of the hunter. Apart from heavy breathing, no noise is made during a 'playfight'. Combatant stallions, on the other hand, are reported to have a very loud battle call.

True animosity between stallions may develop gradually. They may meet repeatedly and try to intimidate each other without actually fighting. Then, suddenly and without warning, one of them attacks the other, mouth wide open showing his teeth. The second stallion has no choice but to rear to evade the attack and avoid injury to his head and neck. For a fraction of a second he has the upper hand; he is now in a position to drop his weight on his opponent and try to grab the top of his assailant's head with his teeth. Before he

The risk of death in battle is as small for stallions as the risk of death in giving birth is for a mare. (Lippizaner stallions in Hungary.)

has time to do so, the other stallion also rears. If he is fast enough, he can throw himself between the kicking front legs and grab his opponent's throat. However, if he fears the power of the kicks, the two will now engage in a veritable boxing contest with their front hooves. As they keep their distance from each other, the danger of injury is relatively small. The situation changes when one horse turns and kicks with his hind legs. These kicks are forceful and well aimed, the head and legs of the opponent being the target.

The fight ends as suddenly as it began. If the two separate following a frenzied pawing and posturing, the battle has probably not been decided – they will meet again. The dispute is concluded when one of them realizes the futility of his attempts to gain the upper hand or when one of them beats the other in combat and chases him off. Premature submission benefits a weaker opponent, as these duels hold a high risk of injury. Vulnerable areas, such as the lips and ears, are easily damaged and deep flesh wounds on neck, croup or flank are prone to infection. Broken bones are the most dangerous injury. Broken ribs can heal, but a broken leg or jaw amounts to a death sentence. The rare occurrence of death following a fight shows how well horses are able to judge their own abilities and those of their opponent.

FRIENDSHIP

Throughout their lives horses form friendships with one or two other animals, but their preferred partner changes as they develop. A foal, of course, has a close relationship with its mother. As it becomes older, brothers and sisters become more important to it. Later, having left its family, it builds relationships with its peers. Young stallions prefer other stallions, mares other young mares. Adults stay true to their chosen partners. Only through death, theft of a mare or replacement of a leading stallion can change be forced. For a mare, the cycle is completed when her first foal is born. Her most important partners from now on will always be her stallion and her youngest offspring. The development of a stallion is completed when he forms a harem. From now on, his mares are his most important partners. As owner of a harem, the stallion has control over his mares, but ownership is really too strong a word. His relationship with the mares shows the same characteristics as the relationships between young animals and between a mother and her foal. The terms 'friendship', 'faithfulness' and 'chosen partnership' are all a means of saying the same thing – a close relationship between two horses. The most important factor in a relationship such as this is time – time spent together. Never losing sight of one another, day and night,

Friendly contact between young Haflinger stallions in the Tyrol.

for years on end when they are adults, they while away the time at the side of their friends. Regardless of their activity – grazing, resting or dustbathing – they are never far apart. If they are separated, they call for each other and do not rest until they are together once again. Standing next to each other and rubbing their heads against each other, they fend off irritating insects.

This knowledge enables you, the rider or even the lucky horse-owner, to be your horse's 'chosen partner'. For people to whom the horse has always been more than just a riding animal, the following advice will not be news. Although you may not be aware of it, your intuitive behaviour towards your horse is in keeping with the social rules that horses follow in the wild. In this case, too, much time needs to be spent with the horse to become a partner. A horse living in a natural group does, after all, want to graze with its friends and not alone. Go for walks with the horse on its halter – friendly horses, too, follow each other around. Hold still when it rubs is head against your shoulder: perhaps it does not want to rid itself of a horsefly or its bridle, but is indicating trust and showing that it likes you. Take the place of its horse partner and ruffle its withers or its back. It will understand your intention. If the horse leaves the other grazing animals when it sees you coming, even though you are not holding a piece of sugar, you have won. Its greatest proof of trust would be a siesta at your side. As you know, a friendship is for life and is based on mutual trust. With any luck your friendship with the horse will last a lifetime.

RIGHT
Regardless of age, horses, like these two Lippizaner mares from Lipica, always seek the company of a few select companions.

OVERLEAF
These two friends (Frisian stallions) from the Altmannschert estate in Germany) might go in search of mares together if they were in the wild.

PAGES 118-119
To nibble each other's coats is an expression of friendship. (Tyrolean blood mares.)

THE HORSE:
ANIMAL OF FLIGHT

To survive in the wild, a horse has to be able to run for its life – its only defence against predators is speed. To leave danger behind as quickly as possible it will run. With its short, stiff back, high hocks, relatively inflexible legs, large nostrils allowing a high air intake and an excellent blood supply to the muscles it is perfectly adapted for that purpose. Donkeys, on the other hand, have more flexible legs which improves their ability to cope with mountainous terrain. Horses can see into the distance to look for approaching predators, as well as keeping an eye open in their immediate vicinity to watch their step, avoid obstacles on the ground or to look for food. They see a lot, but they do not necessarily see it clearly.

Horses' eyes are among the largest in the animal kingdom. The distance between retina and lens and the circumference of the retina are also exceptionally large. Their ability to see in low light or at night is far superior to our own. The position of their eyes on the sides of their head, combined with the large circumference of the retina, enables them to see a large proportion of their surroundings. Each eye can capture an angle of 215° horizontally and 178° vertically. Their field of vision overlaps in front of the face by 60-70°, giving them three-dimensional vision in that area.

Despite their ability to see objects in front of, beside and behind them without turning their heads, horses could do with spectacles, because they suffer from astigmatism. The eye's unevenly-shaped lens distorts the image which they see. They correct this fault by slightly lifting their heads until the image of the object is projected on to an area of the retina where it is sharply focused. One area of the retina is specialized for recognizing movement, but, as re-

After thousands of years of domestication, horses still flee at the first sign of danger. (Andalusian stallion in Spain.)

PREVIOUS PAGE
With a powerful gallop this Andalusian stallion tries to climb a sand dune to gain a better view of his surroundings.

focusing from close to distant vision is difficult, a horse will sooner flee at the first sight of an unknown object and determine its nature afterwards. When a predator threatens, the slightest hesitation can lead to death. Sometimes a horse will shy away from an object that seems to be animated, as it appears in and leaves the horse's field of vision through the movement of its own head.

If a horse looks at an object directly in front of it, its surrounding vision is unclear and vice versa. The best and farthest vision is achieved by raising the head and alternately looking ahead and to the side. This posture is adopted when a horse becomes aware of something unusual. The ears move in all directions to identify any noise. If he considers the disturbance worthy of caution, the leading stallion neighs or snorts, which warns the other horses, if his posture has not already alerted them. Nostrils wide open and muscles taut, the stallion takes a few steps towards the cause of his disquiet. Meanwhile, the other members of his group move closer together and position themselves behind him. If the disturbance proves to be harmless, the stallion turns around and the group moves away together. After 50-100 metres (160-325 ft), they stop to observe their surroundings once again. To avoid dissipating their energy needlessly, they adjust their speed according to the nature of the danger. Unknown or seemingly dangerous objects in the distance are evaded at a walking or trotting pace; if they are surprised by a disturbance close by, they flee in a fast gallop, dispersing in all directions in the process. In open terrain, they regroup only after they have gained a safe distance.

The only remaining predators horses have in the wild are pumas and wolves. They will also flee from bears, although these are not their natural adversaries.

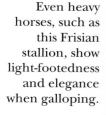

Even heavy horses, such as this Frisian stallion, show light-footedness and elegance when galloping.

OVERLEAF
The particularly agile Haflinger horses even enjoy running about in the snow.

Pumas actually hunt deer, but can, like the coyote, present danger to weak, ill or deserted foals. Packs of wolves sometimes hunt even adult horses, but they usually prefer reindeer, bison or domestic cattle.

Compared to horses, zebras lead a more dangerous life; their enemies include hyena, leopards, lions and cheetahs. On open grassland, they often follow the example of antelopes and wildebeest, who share the savanna with them, and flee when they do. Like a horse, a Hartmann or mountain zebra stallion stands between the potential source of danger and his group and is the last to take flight. Like horses, zebra stallions warn their group with a snort – Hartmann zebras also warn with a short, rasping bark. Grevy zebras, whose stable groups consist of only a mother and her foal, stand a better chance of evading an assailant if they form larger herds. A single zebra is easier prey for a lion than a zebra in a larger herd. The huge herds of wildebeest – the preferred sustenance of all the large African predators – provide even more protection for the zebras. If they join the wildebeest, they are less likely to fall prey than they are if they merely form groups with other zebras. Most zebras choose this method of avoiding predators, but have to pay a price. The large numbers of wildebeest eat up to 80 per cent of the available food, of which the zebras, not being ruminants, need more. To compensate for this disadvantage, they stay at the front of the herd where the ground has not yet been grazed. A further problem is posed by the many calves born among the wildebeest during the rainy season; this attracts predators who are also dangerous to them. When food is in short supply at the start of the dry season, the zebras leave the wildebeest to form groups of exclusively their own kind; they no longer compete for food with the wildebeest, but stand an increased risk of falling prey to a hunter. The dry season is particularly dangerous to their foals. In exceptionally dry conditions, the mothers sometimes travel over long distances to the nearest watering hole, only returning hours later. In the meantime, their foals are left behind with other defenceless foals. Predators and a shortage of food can account for a death rate of 70 per cent among the foals of the Grevy zebra during such times.

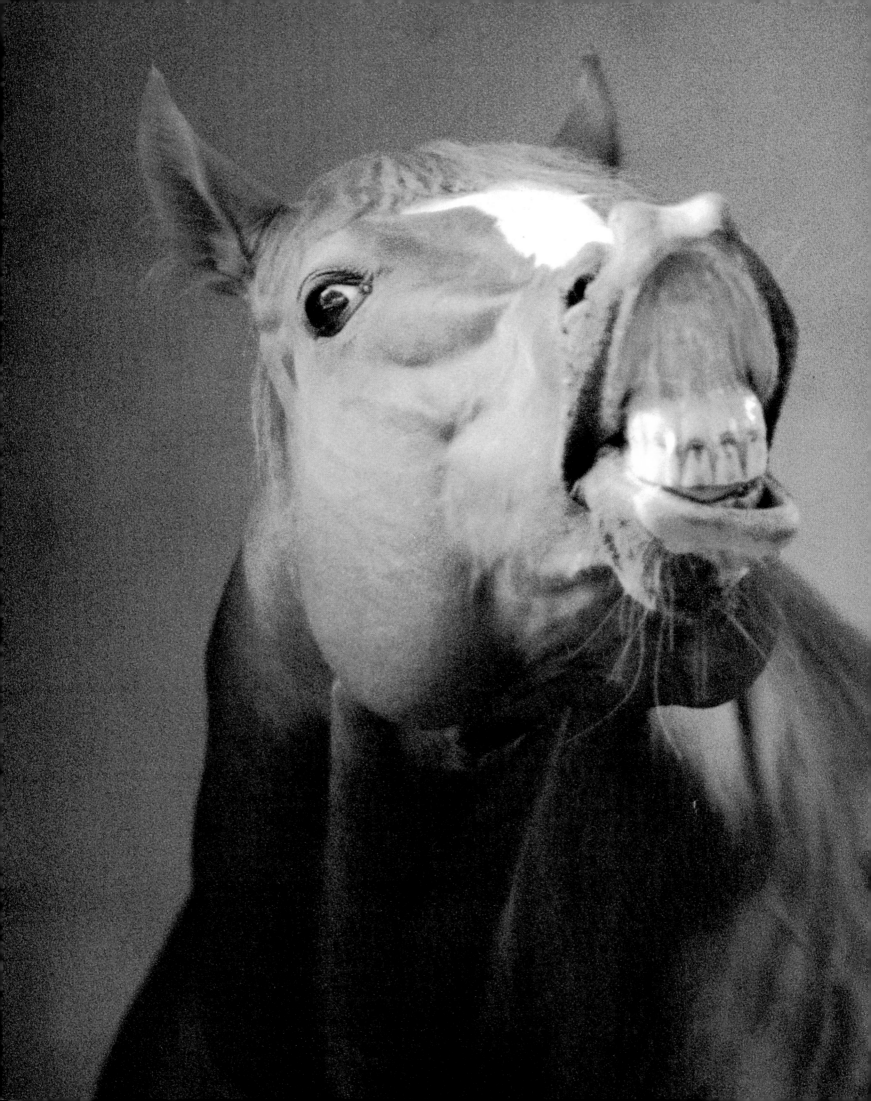

FACIAL
EXPRESSIONS

RIGHT
The faces of these
Shagya-Arab
mares in Hungary
express extreme
vigilance.

Horses are capable of a wide variety of facial expressions, which they combine with a range of postures to communicate with each other. To recognize the individual expressions and to know in which situations they are used enables the observer to understand how the horses relate to each other and to us. When horses meet, we can recognize friendship, superiority, rivalry, protection, caring and much more, both from the way in which they approach each other and from their expressions. Many facial expressions are reflexive; in other words, young animals use them from birth without first having to learn them. Expressions and gestures are usually clear enough to eliminate all ambiguity, leaving no doubt as to their meaning. Nevertheless, misinterpretations do occur. A horse can get a big fright if an animal grazing next to it suddenly swings its head to chase off a horsefly. Even though its ears are not laid back and the swing of the head is not aimed at a specific target, the movement resembles a threatening action. A stamp with the rear leg, again intended to fend off an irritating insect, can also be construed as a threatening action by a nearby horse.

If something attracts a horse's attention, it throws its head in the air and looks, unmoving and with heightened senses, for potential danger. Nostrils flared, it sniffs the air. Horses have an exceptionally well-developed sense of smell. The nostrils lead to a large nose, which separates into many small chambers. The mucous membrane of the nose contains closely packed olfactory cells, which enable the stallion to smell a mare on heat from a distance. Their noses are said to be capable of locating water from far away. If they want to examine a smell in close detail, they fleer, producing a characteristic grimace.

Not a laughing Noriket stallion, but a yawning one. (Dolomites, Italy.)

The nostrils are held close to the source of the scent, then the neck is stretched and the head held high up in the air; at the same time, mouth closed, the upper lip is rolled back until the nostrils are as good as shut. This opens access to the Jacobson organ, which is located at the base of the nasal cavity. The air is inhaled via two blind channels and can, with the help of this organ, be inspected for subtle traces of odour. After this intensive assessment the nose drips. Among adult horses it is usually the stallions who fleer; they do this most frequently during the reproductive season after smelling a mare's urine. Tobacco smoke, the first contact with an unknown food and plants with a particularly strong and potent smell can also invoke fleering.

Although communication is mainly visual, horses also use a variety of sounds to communicate with each other. Horses can hear a wider range of frequencies than humans. Furthermore, their long necks and movable ears enable them not only to hear sounds coming from all directions, but also to pinpoint these fairly accurately. The calls of each horse can be distinguished by its tone, strength and variation of vibration. This enables neighing horses to recognize each other from a distance or without visual contact. Oral communication between social partners, such as stallion and mare, or mare and offspring, are

PREVIOUS PAGE
A hearty yawn often signals the end of the siesta. (Young stallion in the Camargue.)

OVERLEAF
Frisian stallions from the Krefeld stud farm testing scent at a urinating place.

An Arab mare from
Andalusia calling
for her foal.

short, of low frequency and are repeated many times. The greater the distance between the animals, the higher and louder the calls become. They neigh at a familiar horse when it leaves and greet it with a whinny when it returns. During the courtship ritual, stallions grunt, while mares squeal. Squealing is also common among stallions during a demonstration of rank.

Laid-back ears are a threatening gesture. Depending on the strength of the threat, the ears are either just pointed back or pressed right back against the head. At the same time, the nostrils contract, the mouth is pulled back and the facial muscles are tensed. Sometimes the white of the eyes is shown. When an animal opens its mouth and shows its teeth, the threat is to be taken more seriously. If the other horse does not evade, it will be bitten. The threatening face announces a kick from the hind legs. Mares kick more frequently than stallions, who usually approach their opponents head first to attack by biting and rearing. Young stallions sometimes kick as a last resort, before they flee from an older stallion. When a stallion wants to herd his mares together, he makes a threatening face combined with a special posture – he lowers his head almost to the ground, keeping his neck stretched, and moves it from left to right to indicate the direction in which he wants them to go.

TOP
Being threatened by the mare, this Haflinger foal shows its submissive expression.

BOTTOM
Mouth wide open and teeth exposed – the ultimate expression of threat. (Attacking pony stallion in the former Czechoslovakia.)

With its mouth wide open, teeth exposed and eyes closed, a horse appears to be laughing; but it is, in fact, yawning. Horses usually yawn after a rest or when they have just rolled on the ground. Presumably to wind down, stallions will sometimes yawn after copulating or at the end of a confrontation with a rival stallion.

One of the strangest and most conspicuous expressions is chewing, used mainly by young animals to show their submissiveness. Heads lowered, they open their mouths to show their incisors and move their lower jaws up and down; their legs bend slightly and their tails are drawn between the hind legs. Foals show this face when they are threatened by strange animals. Young stallions adopt this posture when they cross the path of or greet a leading stallion. This demeanour usually achieves the desired effect with adults: their aggression is curtailed or evaporates altogether.

Sometimes this posture and expression demonstrate a general apprehension rather than inferiority of rank. Foals often when they are anxious or afraid, for example before an awkward obstacle, such as a water-filled ditch or when they pass strange horses adopt this 'chewing' action.

OVERLEAF
In this crowd, the animal in the middle has only one choice to evade its assailant – to rear. (Group of young Lippizaners in Hungary.)

THANKS

My work on this book, which has taken me 12 years, was supported by many people, to whom I owe my gratitude.

I thank Dr. H.C.W. Georg Olms, President of the International Asil-Club for his help and support with photographic work on his Asil-Arab-Hamasa Stud Farm, and Mrs. Barb Müller for her help on the Hamasa Stud Farm.

I am grateful to Dr. Jaromir Oulehla, Director of the Spanish Riding School in Vienna and the National Lippizaner Stud Farm of Piber for their support of my work. In Hungary, I give special thanks to stud-farm manager Mr. Andor Dallos and the Minister of Forestry and Agriculture, Dr. Janos Ott, as well as to Mr. Ivan Thomka, Mr. Nagy Laszlo and Mr. Czopo Gyula.

My sincerest thanks extend to the family of Doris and Andreas Schmidt from Upper Austria for their help, and to the Tonte family in Vienna. In the Tyrol, my special thanks go to Mr. Otto Schweisgut, Mr. Hannes Schweisgut, Mrs. Ilse Benedetto-Schweisgut, Mr. Reinhold Prandstätter and Mrs. Evelin Swarowski. In Czechoslovakia, I thank Dr. Norbert Zális and Miss Barbora Ciháková (in particular for the photograph on pages 140-1). For help during photography of the Friesan horses, I thank Mr. Bernd Reisgies, Chairman of the German Institute of Breeders and Friends of Friesan Horses, Mr. Hanns-Günther Fröhlich, Mrs. Susanne Rappenecker and Christa and Hans-Joachim Dannenfelser.

In Andalusia, I thank Mr. Miguel Angel Cardenas Osuna for his support of my work, as well as his employees, Mr. Miquel Osuna Saaveda, Mr. Fernando Gago Gorcia and Mr. Juan Manuel Uriquijo Novales; in England, the employees of Chevely Park in Newmarket; in France Dr. Luc Hoffmann – founder of the Biological Station La Tour du Valat – and his associates; further I want to thank for their help Dr. Wolfgang Cranz, Director of the National Stud Farm Marbach and Mr. Andrej Franetic, Director of the Stud Farm of Lipica in the former Yugoslavia. In Weitersfelden, my thanks go to the Diesenreiter family for their constant and sincere support with all the work related to this project.

Lída Jahn-Micek
Weitersfelden, August 1990

A NOTE ABOUT THE PHOTOGRAPHY

I am a Canon-photographer. Ever since I started to work as a photographer, I have used Canon cameras. The following photographic equipment was used for the photography in this book: Cameras: Canon EF, Canon A1 with automatic winding mechanism, Canon T90. Lenses: FD 200mm, Canon FD-Zoom 100-300mm, Canon FD-Zoom 28-85mm. I have used Kodak and Fuji film.

This Asil-Arab stallion fleers after smelling the urine of a mare – a form of behaviour rarely shown by mares.

In 1973, following the suggestion of Professor B. Tschanz (University of Bern), a group of Camargue horses was released on 300 hectares of land on the Tour de Valat estate, which is owned by Dr. L. Hofmann. The aim was to study the behaviour of this herd in natural conditions. Numerous researchers ventured to undertake this painstaking task: P. Duncan, C. Feh, C. Frey-Niggli, B. Michel, A.-M. Monard, E. Murbach, B. Tschanz and S. Wells. All Camargue horses depicted in this book are of that herd, which, incidentally, still exists today. American researchers, having observed wild Mustangs for many years, have also made a sizeable contribution to the understanding of the social behaviour of horses: J. Berger, L. Boyd, D. McCullough, R. Denniston, J. Feist and R. Miller. H. Klingel's work about zebras was continued and developed by J. Ginsberg, E. Joubert, B. Penzhorn and A. Sinclair. They all have contributed to the fascinating insight into the life of horses, which I have tried to describe in this book. My special thanks go to Claudia Feh, who has proof-read the manuscript, and my Camargue horse Juanito, which has chosen me as one of its special partners.

Beatrice Michel